2 to 22 DAYS IN NORWAY, SWEDEN, AND DENMARK

THE ITINERARY PLANNER
1991 Edition

RICK STEVES

John Muir Publications
Santa Fe, New Mexico

Originally published as *22 Days in Norway, Sweden, and Denmark*

Other JMP travel guidebooks by Rick Steves
Asia Through the Back Door (with John Gottberg)
Europe Through the Back Door
Europe 101: History, Art, and Culture for the Traveler
  (with Gene Openshaw)
Mona Winks: Self-Guided Tours of Europe's Top Museums
  (with Gene Openshaw)
22 Days in Europe
2 to 22 Days in Great Britain
22 Days in Germany, Switzerland, and Austria
22 Days in Spain and Portugal

Thanks to Dave Hoerlein and my wife, Anne, for research help and support. Thanks also to Thor, Berit, Hanne, Geir, Hege and Kari-Anne, our Norwegian family.

John Muir Publications, P.O. Box 613, Santa Fe, NM 87504

Steves, Rick, 1955–
    2 to 22 days in Norway, Sweden, and Denmark : the itinerary
planner / Rick Steves. — 1991 ed.
       p.   cm.
    Rev. and updated ed. of: 22 days in Norway, Sweden & Denmark.
c1988.
    Includes index.
    ISBN 0-945465-87-4
    1. Scandinavia—Description and travel—1981-   —Guide-books.
I. Steves, Rick, 1955–   22 days in Norway, Sweden & Denmark.
II. Title.   III. Title: Two to twenty-two days in Norway, Sweden,
and Denmark.
DL4.S74   1991
914.804'88—dc20   90-28566
                                                                              CIP

Design Mary Shapiro
Maps Dave Hoerlein
Cover Map Tim Clark
Typography Copygraphics, Santa Fe, New Mex.
Printer McNaughton & Gunn, Inc., Saline, Mich.

Distributed to the book trade by
W. W. Norton & Company, Inc.

CONTENTS

Southern Scandinavia

HOW TO USE THIS BOOK

This book is the tour guide in your pocket. It lets you be the boss by giving you the best 2 to 22 days in Scandinavia and a suggested way to use that time most efficiently.

Our 2 to 22 Days series is for do-it-yourselfers who would like the organization and smoothness of a tour without the straitjacket. It's almost like having your "Danish" and eating it too.

This plan is maximum thrills per mile, minute, and dollar. It's designed for travel by rental car but is adaptable to train (see pp. 170-174). The pace is fast but not hectic. It's designed for the American with limited time who wants to see everything but who doesn't want the "if it's Tuesday this must be Bergen" craziness. The plan includes the predictable "required" biggies (Tivoli Gardens, Hans Christian Andersen's house, and the Little Mermaid) with a good dose of "Back Door" intimacy mixed in—a bike tour of a sleepy remote Danish isle, a stranded time-passed fjord village, and a look at a failed communal utopia.

The "22 Days" books originated (and are still used) as handbooks for those who join me on my "Back Door Europe" tours.

Since most large organized tours work to keep their masses ignorant while visiting many of the same places we'll cover, this book is handy for anyone taking a typical big bus tour—but wanting also to maintain some independence and flexibility.

This *2 to 22 Days in Norway, Sweden, and Denmark* plan is balanced and streamlined. To prevent typical tourist burn-out, I've included only the most exciting castles and churches. I've been very selective. For example, we won't visit both the Open-Air Folk Museum in Oslo and in Lillehammer, but we will visit the better of the two. The "better," of course, is only my opinion. But after fifteen busy years of travel writing, lecturing, tour guiding, and filming my PBS TV series, I've developed a sixth sense of what tickles the traveler's fancy. I love this itinerary. Just thinking about it makes me smell like goat cheese.

Of course, connect-the-dots travel isn't perfect, just as color-by-numbers painting isn't good art. But this book is your smiling Swede, your Nordic navigator. It's your well thought out and tested itinerary. I've done it—and refined it—many times on my own and with groups (most recently in July and August 1990). Use it, take advantage of it, but don't let it rule you.

Read this book before you begin your trip. Use it as a rack to hang more ideas on. As you plan, study, travel, and talk to people, fill this book with notes. It's your tool. The book is adaptable to any Scandinavian trip. It could be your blueprint for a one-week blitz tour of the capitals, or you could easily use it to fill a 30-day trip. You'll find 22 rearrangeable units, or days, each built with the same sections:

1. **Introductory overview** for the day.

2. An hour-by-hour **suggested schedule** recommended for that day.

3. List of the most important **sightseeing highlights** (rated: ▲▲▲ Don't miss; ▲▲ Try hard to see; ▲ Worthwhile if you can make it).

4. **Transportation** tips and instructions.

5. **Food and Accommodations**: How and where to find the best budget places, including addresses, phone numbers, and my favorites.

6. **Orientation** and easy-to-read **maps** locating all recommended places.

7. **Helpful hints** on shopping, transportation, day-to-day chores.

8. **Itinerary options** for those with more or less than the suggested time, or with particular interests. As the book's title suggests, this itinerary is rubbery!

Maps

My mapmaker and research assistant, Dave Hoerlein, knows a good map is worth a thousand words. His maps go hand in glove with my text. They are designed to orient you and direct you until you pick up something better at the tourist information office. Dave points out all the major landmarks, streets, and accommodations mentioned in the book and indicates the best city entry and exits for our 22-day plan.

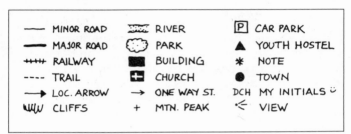

—— MINOR ROAD	▨ RIVER	P CAR PARK
—— MAJOR ROAD	☁ PARK	▲ YOUTH HOSTEL
++++ RAILWAY	▧ BUILDING	✳ NOTE
---- TRAIL	✚ CHURCH	● TOWN
→● LOC. ARROW	→ ONE WAY ST.	DCH MY INITIALS ⌣
⋓⋓ CLIFFS	+ MTN. PEAK	⤺ VIEW

Travel Smart

Lay departure groundwork upon arrival in a town, read a day ahead in this book, use the local tourist information offices, and enjoy the hospitality of the Scandinavian people. Ask questions. Most locals are eager to point you in their idea of the right direction. Use the telephone, wear a money belt, use a small pocket notebook to organize your thoughts, and make simplicity a virtue. If you insist on being confused, your trip will be a mess. Those who expect to travel smart, do.

Cost

Scandinavia is Europe's most expensive corner. Remember, you're not getting less for your travel dollar. Up here there are just no lousy or cheap alternatives to classy, cozy, sleek Scandinavia. Electronic eyes flush youth hostel toilets; public telephones have volume controls. Travel here can be reasonable. If you're really on the ball, you can keep your daily costs to around $50 (plus transportation).

Trip costs for 22 days break down like this: A basic round-trip U.S.A.-Copenhagen flight costs $500 to $1,000 (depending on the season and where you fly from). Figure about $600 for a three-week car rental (split between two people, $700 for rent including tax and insurance, and about $500 for gas) or about $500 for three weeks of rail and bus travel. For room and board, figure $50 a day, double occupancy—$1,100. Budgeting for $60 doubles including breakfasts, $5 lunches, and $15

dinners, this is more than feasible, and if necessary, you
can travel cheaper (see my book, *Europe Through the
Back Door*, for the skills and tricks of budget travel). Add
$400 or so for admissions and fun money and you've got
yourself a great Scandinavian adventure for under $3,000.

Those with limited budgets must study this book. It
will save you a fortune. Read it carefully from start to finish. Many of the general skills and cheap tricks used in
Copenhagen work in Oslo as well. Scandinavia can be
brutal on the budget or a breeze, depending on your skills.

Accommodations

Accommodation expenses will make or break your
budget. There are plenty of decent $15 per bed alterna-
tives to hotels, and an overall average of $60 per night per
double is easy using this book's listings. Unless otherwise
noted, the accommodations I've listed will hold a room
with a phone call until 6:00 p.m. with no deposit, and the
proprietors speak English. I like places that are small, central, clean, traditional, friendly, and not listed in other
guidebooks. Most places listed meet five of these six
virtues.

Tourist Offices: Every city we'll visit has an energetic
and well-organized tourist office whose room-finding
service is a great money saver, well worth the small fee.
Be very clear about what you want. (Say "CHEAP," and
whether you have sheets or a sleeping bag, will take a
twin or double, don't require a shower, etc.) They know
the hotel quirks and private room scene better than any-
body. And they are working for you. Price listings are
often misleading since they omit cheaper oddball rooms
and special clearance deals.

To save substantial money, bring your own sheet or
sleeping bag like Scandinavian travelers do and always
offer to provide it in cheap accommodations. Especially
in rural areas, this can save $10 per person per night. And
to get even more sleep for your dollar, pull the dark
shades to keep out the very early morning sun.

Hotels: These are very expensive ($60 to $150 doubles) with some exceptions. Business class hotels dump

prices to attract tourists in summer and on weekend (Friday, Saturday, or Sunday) evenings. Certain hotel cards or passes do the same thing in a more organized way. Norway's Fjord Pass, the Scandia Bonus Pass, and the Scandinavia Holiday Pass offer 15 to 50 percent discounts at major hotels in summer only—ask your travel agent for specifics. If you'll normally be using hotels, these can be worthwhile, although I don't bother since I find it cheapest to arrive without a reservation and let the local tourist offices match or even beat the special card or discount pass prices. Hotels are expensive, but the bill includes a large (and otherwise expensive) breakfast.

Hostels: Scandinavian hostels are Europe's finest. They offer many classy facilities, members' kitchens, cheap and hot meals, plenty of private "family" rooms, great people experiences, and they have no age restrictions. Many are closed in the off-season. Buy a membership card before you leave home. Nonmembers are normally welcome for an extra charge ($5 a night). Bring a bed sheet from home or plan on renting them for about $5 a night. (Nonmembers without sheets save little in hostels over hotels.) You'll find lots of Volvos, Saabs, and BMWs in the YH parking lots, as the Scandinavians know hostels provide the best $15 beds in town. (See the listing in the Appendix.)

For even cheaper beds, use the new mattress-on-the-floor network of "Interpoint" accommodations in Scandinavia's big cities. These YMCA-run sleep-ins require a one-time 20 kr membership, available on the spot.

Camping: Scandinavia offers some of Europe's top campgrounds. It's a very practical, comfortable, and actually cheap way to go ($5 per person with camping card, available on the spot). Each national tourist office has a fine brochure/map listing all their campgrounds. This is the middle-class Scandinavian family way to travel: safe, great social fun, no reservation problems. Free camping is permitted and is easy in Sweden and Norway (but not allowed in Denmark).

Huts: Most campgrounds provide huts (Hytter) for noncampers who want in on this cheap alternative to

hotels. Huts normally sleep four to six and charge one fee
(around $25) plus extra if you need sheets or blankets.
Each hut has firm bunks and a kitchenette. While these
are well worth looking into, many are booked in summer
long in advance. Locals typically move in for a week or two.

Private Rooms: Throughout Scandinavia, people
earn a few extra crowns by renting rooms. While some
put out a "Rom," "Rum," or "Hus Rum" sign, most operate solely through the local tourist office. In some cases,
the tourist information offices (TIs) put you in contact
with these homes only when all the hotels are full. Prices
are set by the TI—normally about $35 per double—and
these are a fantastic value as well as an opportunity to
make some local friends. You'll get your own key and a
lived-in, clean, and comfortable but usually simple private room with free access to the family shower and W.C.
Booking direct saves both you and your host the cut the
tourist office takes. Before you conclude that these are
impossibly cheap, remember, this is one form of income
that the Scandinavian tax man has a tough time getting
his impressively hungry fingers on.

Reservations

If you like to pave the road, you'll travel with reservations
in advance. You can book your entire trip (ideally about
six weeks in advance) on the phone from home in about
an hour for about $50. Nearly all accommodations listed
will hold a room with a quick telephone call if you follow
this procedure: try to call in the wee American hours
(cheapest rates, morning in Scandinavia, midnight on the
West Coast is ideal); tell them your name, how many you
are, how many nights you need, and when you'll arrive; if
they have rooms available, check the price and how late
they'll hold the room that day with no money deposited;
accept the room and promise to send a letter confirming
this reservation; in the letter ask for a confirmation letter
in return and promise to telephone a day or two before
you plan to arrive. It doesn't hurt to tell them you're a 2 to
22 Days reader. Keep careful track of reservations made.

It's no problem to cancel. But it's a big problem if you just don't show up. Please, I've promised my hotel friends that my readers are more reliable than the average American traveler in this regard. In return, they agree to hold a room with no deposit until at least late in the afternoon of the day you'll arrive. (If you need to arrive too late, "plan" to arrive early and reassure them with phone calls the day of your late arrival.) Not having to send deposits makes your trip a lot more flexible and simple.

Food
The smartest budget travelers do as the Scandinavians do—avoid restaurants. Prepared food is heavily taxed, and the local cuisine just isn't worth trip bankruptcy. Of course, you'll want to take an occasional splurge into each culture's high cuisine, but the "high" refers mostly to the price tag. Why not think of eating on the road as eating at home without your kitchen. Get creative with cold food and picnics. Daily restaurant eating is unnatural. I eat well on a budget in Scandinavia with the following approach.

Breakfast: Breakfast is a huge and filling buffet when included in the hotel room price. It's normally a 35-50 kr option. This includes: cereal or porridge, "let" (lowfat) or "sod" (whole) milk or various kinds of drink yogurt (it's proper to pour the yogurt in the bowl and sprinkle the crispy cereal over it); bread, crackers, cheese (the brown stuff is goat's cheese; your trip will go much better when you develop a taste for this stuff), cold cuts, and jam; fruit; juice and coffee or tea. Most places will fill a coffee addict's thermos for about $3. Some places almost encourage you to take a sandwich away for lunch. I bring a baggie to breakfast and leave with a light lunch—sandwich and apple or can of yogurt. Yes, I know, this is nearly stealing, but here's how I rationalize it. Throughout my trip, I'm paying lots of taxes to support a social system that my host (but not me) will enjoy; I could have eaten what I take at that all-you-can-eat sitting but choose to finish breakfast elsewhere. . . later; the Vikings did much worse things than that; and everybody's doing it (notice how a huge bowl of apples disappears and there's not a core in sight). After a big breakfast, a light baggie lunch fits nicely into a busy sightseeing day.

If you skip your hotel's breakfast, you can visit a bakery and get a sandwich and cup of coffee. The only cheap breakfast is one you make yourself. Many simple accommodations provide kitchenettes, or at least electric coffee pots.

Lunch: Scandinavians aren't big on lunch, often just grabbing a sandwich (*smorrebrod*) and a cup of coffee at their work desk. Follow suit with a quick picnic or a light meal at a sandwich shop or snack bar.

Picnic! Scandinavia has colorful markets and even cheaper supermarkets. After hours you'll find mini-markets at gas and train stations most helpful. Some shopping tips: Wasa cracker bread ("Sport" is my favorite, "Ideal" flatbrod is ideal for in-the-car munchies), prepackaged meat and cheese, goat cheese (geitost; "ekte" means pure and stronger), yogurt, freshly cooked fish in markets, fresh fruit and vegetables, lingonberries, mustard and sandwich spreads (shrimp, caviar) in a squeeze tube, boxes of juice, milk, pytt i panna (Swedish hash), rye bread (look for "rag," sweet as cake). If you're lazy, most places offer cheap ready-made sandwiches. If you're bored, most places have hot chicken, salads by the portion, fresh and cheap liver pate, and other ways to get away from sandwiches.

Dinners: The large meal of the Nordic day is an early dinner. Alternate between cheap, unmemorable but filling cafeteria or fast food dinners ($10) and atmospheric, carefully chosen restaurants popular with locals ($18). One main course and two salads or soups fills two travelers without emptying their pocketbooks. The cheap eateries close early because in Scandinavia a normal, practical, fill-the-tank dinner is eaten early, usually around 5:00 or 6:00 p.m. Anyone eating out late is dining, will linger longer, and expect to pay much more. A $15 Scandinavian meal is not that much more than a $10 American meal since tax and tip are included in the menu price. In most Scandinavian restaurants, you can ask for more potatoes or vegetables, so any restaurant entrée is

basically an all-you-can-eat deal. Fast food joints, pizzerias, Chinese food, and salad bars are inexpensive. Booze
will break you. Drink water (served free with an understanding smile at any restaurant), buy the liquor duty-
free, or take out a loan. Waitresses are well paid and tips
are normally included, although it's polite to round up
the bill.

Most nations have one inedible dish that is cherished
with a perverse but patriotic sentimentality. These dishes
often originate with a famine and are kept in use to
remind the young of their forefathers' suffering. Norway's penitential food, lutefisk (dried cod marinated for
several days in potash and water), is used for Christmas
and jokes.

When to Go
Summer is best. Scandinavia bustles and glistens under
the July and August sun. Scandinavian schools get out
around June 20, most local industries take July off, and
the British and central Europeans tend to visit Scandinavia in August. You'll notice crowds during these times,
but it's never as crowded as southern Europe and (especially if you call ahead and utilize local information
sources) this tour is easily done without hotel reservations.

"Shoulder season" travel (May, early June, and September) involves minimal crowds, decent weather, and sights
and tourist fun spots still open—but without the vitality
of summer. You can usually just grab a room almost
whenever and wherever you like.

Winter is a bad time to explore Scandinavia. No crowds,
but many sights and accommodations are closed or only
open on a limited schedule. Business travelers drive hotel
prices way up in winter. Winter weather can be cold and
dreary, and nighttime will draw the shades on your sightseeing well before dinner.

Prices and Times
To figure approximate prices in this book: 6 kr = $1. I've
priced things in local currencies throughout the book.

While each of the Scandinavian countries' crowns
(krona) have different values, they are close. I have kept
things simple by figuring one krona is worth 18 cents—
about six in a U.S. dollar. All krona are decimalized—100
ore equals 1 krona. The money is generally not accepted
outside of its home turf (except, of course, at foreign
exchange services and banks). Standard abbreviations
are: Danish krona—DKK, Swedish krona—SEK, and
Norwegian krona—NOK. We'll keep it simple and use the
krona abbreviation, kr, for Denmark, Sweden, and Norway. To translate any prices in krona into U.S. dollars, simply divide by 6 (30 kr = $5).

The Finnish markka, FIM, or mk, is worth about 25
cents (4 mk = $1).

I have listed only normal full prices. Scandinavia is
generous with student, youth, and senior discounts—
often 50%. Students should travel with an International
Student Identity Card (ISIC; purchase before you leave
home).

These countries are more stable than most European
countries, but it's always smart to double-check hours
and times when you arrive—especially when traveling
between October and May. Prices, as well as hours, telephone numbers, and so on, are accurate as of late 1990.
Things are always changing, and I've tossed timidity out
the window knowing you'll understand that this book,
like any guidebook, starts to yellow even before it's
printed.

In Scandinavia—and in this book—you'll be using the
24-hour clock (or "military" time). After noon, instead of
p.m. times, you'll see 13:00, 14:00, and so on. (Just sub-
tract 12 and add p.m. to get "normal" time).

The Language Barrier
I've written this book for people who speak only
English—like me. Of course it would be great to speak
the local language, but in Scandinavia, English is all you
need. They say a Scandinavian can speak any language
that will separate a tourist from his money. Whatever the
motive, especially among the young, English is Scandina-

via's foreign language of choice. In fact, English is well on the way to doing to the Scandinavian languages what it did to the old Irish. Learn the polite words and a few very basic phrases (see Appendix) and you'll have absolutely no problems.

Even though small children watch and understand cartoons in English these days, each country does have its own distinct language. Except for Finnish, they are very closely related and have many similarities to English (a cousin of the Nordic tongues). The Scandinavians have several letters (Æ, Å, Ø) that we don't have. To keep things simple in this book, I have opted to spell Scandinavian words with only our letters. This really blows the pronounciation for those who speak these languages. But for you and me, the only possible problem this causes is in alphabetizing. Whenever I can't find something (like the word for the town "Arhus" in the map index), I look after "Z" where they store the special letters of the Nordic alphabet. My apologies to these languages for my laziness.

Borders, Passports, Visas, Shots, and Banking
Traveling throughout this region requires only a passport. No shots, and no visas. Border crossings between Norway, Sweden, Denmark, and Finland are extremely easy. Normally you won't even have to stop. When you change countries, however, you do change money, postage stamps, and more. Local sales taxes are refunded on the spot for souvenirs and gifts purchased. Ask local merchants for instructions.

Banking in Scandinavia can be costly. Generally, the bank rates are consistent and fair, with buying and selling rates within a percent or two of each other. But they really get you with the fee—around $3 for cash and $4 for traveler's checks. Norwegian banks charge $2 or $3 per check, so bring big denominations. While rates are pretty consistent, fees vary greatly. In many cases, small cash exchanges are cheaper outside of banks at places that offer bad rates but no fees (such as exchange desks on international boats).

Stranger in a Strange Land
We travel all the way to Europe to enjoy differences—to
become temporary locals. You may find some frustra-
tions. Certain truths that we find God-given or self-
evident—things like cold beer, a bottomless coffee cup,
long hot showers, and bigger being better—are suddenly
not so true. One of the beauties of travel is the opportunity to see that there are logical, civil, and even better
alternatives. While the fast and materialistic culture of
America is sneaking into these countries in many ways,
simplicity has yet to become subversive. Scandinavians
are into "sustainable affluence." They have experimented
aggressively in the area of socialism—with mixed results.
To travel here tends to pry open one's hometown
blinders. Fit in, don't look for things American on the
wrong side of the Atlantic, and you're sure to enjoy a full
dose of Scandinavian hospitality.

Scheduling and Travel Speed
The overall plan and each daily suggested schedule is
very carefully laid out. But you'll need to fine-tune it to
plug in rest days, avoid closed days, and hit the most festivals and least traffic jams. Play with the calendar. Read
through this book to troubleshoot problems before you
leave home. Stretching the trip to 28 or 30 days would be
luxurious. Minimize one-night stands.

   Many find my tempo is too fast, and, for them, the
day's suggested schedule is impractical. My schedules are
tried and tested. They work but assume you are well
organized, traveling to experience as much as possible,
and plan to rest when you get home. Really—I don't
mind if you slow it down.

Car Rental
If you plan to drive, arrange your rental well before
departure. Car rental is usually cheapest when arranged
in the United States through your travel agent rather than
in Scandinavia. You'll want a weekly rate with unlimited
mileage. Plan to pick up the car in Copenhagen and drop
it off there at the end of your trip. Remember, if you drop

it early or keep it longer, you'll be credited or charged at a fair, prorated price. Each major car rental agency has a Copenhagen Airport office. Comparison shop through your agent and Rafco (see below).

I normally rent nearly the smallest, least expensive model (e.g., Ford Fiesta). For a bigger, roomier, and more powerful inexpensive car, move up to the Ford 1.3-liter Escort or VW Polo category. For peace of mind, I splurge for the CDW insurance (collision damage waiver) which gives a zero-deductible rather than the standard sky-high deductible, buy travel insurance that includes the CDW at a more reasonable price, or use a credit card that includes CDW. Remember, mini-buses are a great budget way to go for 5 to 9 people.

Rafco, a small Danish company near Copenhagen, rents nearly new Peugeots at almost troublemaking prices. Rafco is tied into Thrifty and is super eager to please. The manager, Ken, promises these prices to my readers through 1992 for 22 days, start and finish in Copenhagen, with all tax and unlimited mileage (first figure) and CDW insurance supplement (second figure): tiny Nissan Micra—2,800 kr/400 kr; the okay-for-two Peugeot 205—3,500 kr/ 450 kr; the bigger, four-door Peugeot 309—3,990 kr/660 kr; Peugeot 405 station wagon—5,000 kr/660 kr, similar rates on other models. They also have new small motor homes that are very popular for families on a budget (about $800 a week, with gear, four to five beds, kitchen, WC, and a 10% discount to 2 to 22 Days readers). For more information and their brochure, call or write to Rafco: Energivej 24, DK-2750 Ballerup, Denmark, tel. 45/42 97 15 00, fax 45/44 68 68 22. By the way, Rafco often needs drivers to deliver or return cars between Copenhagen and Paris, Amsterdam, or Frankfurt. Call for the possibility of a free trip.

Driving in Scandinavia
It's very difficult to keep your eyes on the road with all that luscious scenery flying by. You'll see lots of broken guardrails. Other than that, Scandinavia is a great place to drive. All you need is a valid driver's license and a car. Gas

is expensive, around $4 per gallon, roads are good but
nerve-rackingly skinny in West Norway, traffic generally
sparse, drivers sober and civil, signs and road maps excellent, local road etiquette nothing very different, seatbelts
required. Use your headlights day and night; it's required
in most of Scandinavia. Bikes whizz by close and quiet,
so be on guard. There are plenty of good facilities, gas
stations, and scenic rest stops. Snow is a serious problem
off-season in the mountains. Parking is a headache only
in major cities, where expensive garages are safe and
plentiful. Denmark uses a parking windshield clock disk
(free; set it when you arrive, and be back before your
posted time limit is up). Even in the Nordic countries,
thieves break into cars. Park carefully, use the trunk, and
show no stealables.

Never drink and drive—not even one! The laws are
very severe.

Car vs. Train
While this tour is designed for car travel, a chapter in the
back of the book adapts it for train travel. With a few
exceptions, trains cover this entire itinerary wonderfully.
A three-week first-class Eurailpass costs $498. A 21-day
first-class Nordtourist pass, which you buy at any Scandinavian train station, costs about $300 for a 2nd-class
pass. (The first-class Nordtourist is not worth the extra
expense of about $100.) A train pass is best for single
travelers, those who'll be spending more time in big cities
and those who'd rather not drive in Europe. If traveling
by train remember the super efficiency of night travel.
The couchette supplement is worth the extra money.

One or two travel cheaper by train pass, three or more
save by driving. While a car gives you the ultimate in
mobility and freedom, enables you to search for hotels
more easily, and carries your bags for you, the train zips
you effortlessly from city to city, usually dropping you in
the center and near the tourist office. Cars are great in the
countryside but an expensive headache in places like
Oslo, Copenhagen, and Bergen. To go by car or train—
that is the question. And for this itinerary, I'd drive.

Coming to Scandinavia from Europe

There are often cheaper flights from the U.S.A. into
Frankfurt and Amsterdam than into Copenhagen. And
you may be traveling in central Europe before or after
your Scandinavian tour. It's a long, rather dull one-day
drive to Scandinavia from Amsterdam, Frankfurt, and the
castles of the Rhine region (with a two-hour, $50 per car
and passenger ferry crossing at Puttgarten). By train the
trip is effortless—overnight from Amsterdam or Frankfurt. The $100 trip is included with your Eurailpass (but
not the Nordtourist pass).

Compared to other parts of Europe, there's little to get
excited about between Copenhagen and Amsterdam or
Frankfurt. I'd do the trip overnight. Berlin is an easy connection (via the Gedser-Warnemunde boat) overnight by
train from Copenhagen.

Flying in Scandinavia

Since the European airline industry has been deregulated,
there are some surprisingly inexpensive fares within
Scandinavia and from there to Europe. SAS has cheap
summer fares and each country has some round-trip specials. Before buying any long surface transportation
ticket, look into a budget airfare at a local travel agency.
Each capital has agencies that specialize in discount fares.
A $100 one-way flight from Bergen to Copenhagen
wouldn't surprise me, but I wouldn't find it until I got to
Scandinavia.

Recommended Guidebooks

This book is your itinerary handbook. You can do a
smooth and smart trip with this and the help of the local
tourist offices. Even so, consider some supplemental
information. I know it hurts to spend $20 or $30 on extra
books and maps, but when you consider the improve-
ments they'll make in your $2,600 vacation, the informa-
tion is very valuable. In Scandinavia, one good budget tip
can easily save the price of the extra guidebook.

Europe Through the Back Door (by me; Santa Fe, N.M.:
John Muir Publications, 1990) gives you the basic skills,
the foundations that make this demanding 2- to 22-day

plan possible. Chapter topics include minimizing jet lag, packing light, driving versus train travel, finding budget beds without reservations, changing money, theft, travel photography, long distance telephoning in Europe, ugly Americanism, traveler's toilet trauma, laundry, and itinerary strategies and techniques. The book also contains special articles on 40 exciting nooks and undiscovered European crannies that I call "Back Doors."

Europe 101: History and Art for Travelers (by Rick Steves and Gene Openshaw, published by John Muir Publications) tells you about the cultures in a practical, fun-to-read, 360-page package. Ideal for those who want to be able to step into a Gothic cathedral and excitedly nudge their partner saying, "Isn't this a great improvement over Romanesque!"

One reason I wrote this book is because, for my style, there is precious little in the way of good guidebook help available on the Scandinavian countries. Here's a quick rundown:

Arthur Frommer's *Scandinavia on $60 a Day*—This has been the only good budget guide to independent, do-it-yourself Scandinavian travel. The Scandinavia book has lots of helpful ideas, and while it, like any mainstream guide, is short on guts, it's excellent for the less rugged, better financed traveler. Frommer himself writes the *Europe on $40 a Day* book, and the Oslo, Copenhagen, and Stockholm chapters in this book are great for the budget traveler.

Let's Go Europe—My favorite travel guidebook, written by Harvard students, is weak on Scandinavia. Still, its short Nordic chapters are very helpful for the more rugged budget traveler of any age.

The Rough (or Real) Guide to Scandinavia is the bulkiest budget book on the area. Judging by the number of wrong telephone numbers, it took its name too seriously. Still, for historic and cultural background and budget tips, I found it helpful.

There are other guides to Scandinavia published by Baedeker, Fodor, and Rand McNally and guides to Norway and Sweden by Hunter. All are heavy on facts, low on personality and opinion.

Many travelers enjoy Karen Brown's *Scandinavian Country Inns and Manors*, which proposes interesting routes with a focus on elegant little hotels. Her recommended hotels are very charming—though not cheap.

Motoring in Norway, published and sold in Norway, is the best of the Norwegian-published English guides. It's very dry but gives you a running commentary on virtually every tourist route in Norway. Thumb through it in the Oslo tourist office.

Passport Books publishes *Just Enough Scandinavian*, a small phrase book covering Danish, Norwegian, and Swedish. It's the best phrase book of its kind, but the language barrier is microscopic here. A simple English-Norsk dictionary is helpful, but, frankly, you can get by fine with English.

I'd recommend one overall road map for southern Scandinavia (I used the Kummerly and Frey, 1:1,000,000 edition) and a map for "Southern Norway-North" (I used Sor Norge-nord, 1:325,000, by Cappelens Kart). Southern Norway-South is handy, but SN-N is essential. Excellent city and regional maps are available from local TIs, usually for free.

Back Door Manners
As I updated this book, I heard over and over how 2 to 22 Days readers were the most considerate and fun-to-have-as-guests travelers my recommended hotels and private homes dealt with. Thank you for traveling sensitive to the culture and as temporary locals. It's fun to follow you in my travels.

Raise Your Travel Dreams to Their Upright and Locked Position
The goal of this book is to free you, not chain you. Please defend your spontaneity as you would your mother. Use this book to sort Scandinavia's myriad sights into the most interesting, representative, diverse, and efficient 22 days of travel. Use it to avoid time- and money-wasting

mistakes, to get more intimate with Europe by traveling without a tour—as a temporary local person. And use it as a point of departure from which to shape your best possible travel experience.

Anyone who has read this far has what it takes intellectually to do this tour on their own. With the information in this book and a determination to travel smart, you can expect a smooth trip. Be confident, militantly positive, relish the challenge and rewards of doing your own planning. Judging from all the positive feedback and happy postcards we receive from those who traveled with the first edition of this book, it's safe to assume you're on your way to a great Scandinavian vacation— independent, inexpensive, and with the finesse of an experienced traveler.

Send Me a Postcard, Drop Me a Line
While I do what I can to keep this book accurate and up-to-date, things are always changing. If you enjoy a successful trip with the help of this book and would like to share your discoveries (and make my job a lot easier), please send in any tips, recommendations, criticisms, or corrections to me at Europe Through the Back Door, 109 4th N., Box C-2009, Edmonds, WA 98020. All correspondents will receive a two-year subscription to our "Back Door Travel" quarterly newsletter (it's free anyway), and recommendations used will get you a first-class rail pass in heaven. Thanks, and happy travels!

ITINERARY

DAY 1   Your Scandinavian adventure starts in wonderful Copenhagen, the most direct and least expensive Scandinavian capital to fly into from the U.S.A. and the gateway to Scandinavia from points south in Europe. After an evening orientation walk you'll be well acquainted with Denmark's capital.

DAYS 2 and 3   Copenhagen, Scandinavia's largest and most loved city, deserves two very busy days. Climb the church spire, cruise the harbor, follow a local historian on a walk through the old town, browse through Europe's greatest pedestrian shopping mall, enjoy a smorgasbord feast and spend a memorable night at the famous Tivoli Gardens, the Continent's ultimate amusement park. And that's just the beginning of what Copenhagen has to offer.

DAY 4   Pick up your rental car, or validate your rail pass, before leaving Copenhagen to explore the highlights of North Zealand—a great castle and Scandinavia's top modern art museum. Then ferry to Sweden and travel deep into that pristine and woodsy land.

DAY 5   Today is for Smaland. You'll tour the best glass factory in Sweden, cross Europe's longest bridge to hike through the Stonehenge-type mysteries of the strange island of Oland, and bed down in atmospheric old Kalmar, historically the "key to Sweden" and home of a magnificent medieval castle.

DAY 6   Driving north along Sweden's east coast, picnic and take a walk along the romantic Gota Canal before finding your hotel in Stockholm. After going over your Stockholm plans with the very helpful tourist information people, join a local historian for a walk through Stockholm's lantern-lit old town, followed by dinner in an Old World inn.

DAYS 7 and 8   Stockholm, one of Europe's most underrated cities, tempts many to toss out the itinerary and

Scandinavia in 22 Days

move in. Green, built on fourteen islands, surrounded by water and woods, energetic, efficient, and full of history, it demands a busy two days. Crawl through Europe's best-preserved old warship, tour Europe's first and best open-air folk museum, and relax on a canal boat tour. A look at the modern side of this trend-setting city includes its futuristic planned suburbs, art galleries, city hall—host of the annual Nobel Prize banquet—and shopping. On your third Stockholm evening, take Europe's most enjoyable cruise with lovely archipelago scenery, a setting sun, and a royal smorgasbord dinner.

DAY 9   The boat is your hotel and you've got all day to see Finland's neoclassical capital, Helsinki. Catch a half-day city bus tour or just wander through this compact town. Either way you can enjoy Helsinki's ruddy harbor-front market, count goosebumps in her churches, and tour the national museum. By dinnertime you'll once again surround yourself with beautiful islands and lots of food. How about dancing and a sauna before crawling into your stateroom?

DAY 10   Back on Swedish soil you'll visit historic Uppsala. Its cathedral and university are the oldest, largest, tallest, etc., and the compact and bustling little city is a fine morning stop before making the long drive across Sweden and into Oslo, Norway's capital city.

DAYS 11 and 12   Oslo's Viking spirit, past and present, has left sights that tell a thrilling story. Two days here allow plenty of time to prowl through the remains of ancient Viking ships, and more peaceful but equally gutsy modern boats like the *Kon Tiki, Ra*, and *Fram*. You'll hear stirring stories of the local World War II Nazi resistance and trace the country's folk culture at the Norwegian Open-Air Folk Museum. For the modern side of Norway's capital, browse through the new yuppie-style harbor shopping complex, tour its formerly avant-garde city hall, get a good dose of Gustav Vigeland's sculpture, and climb the towering Holmenkollen ski jump.

DAY 13   Heading for the Norwegian hills, past the countryside manor house where Norway's constitution was signed, enjoy Norway's best folk museum, and drive deep into the romantic Gudbrandsdal Valley — Peer Gynt country. Your destination is an ancient log and sod farmstead turned hotel, tucked in a quiet valley under Norway's highest mountains.

DAY 14   After a relaxed morning, drive over Norway's highest mountain pass, deep into Jotunheim ("giant's home") country. A long, rugged road takes you to the slow but fierce tongue of the Nigard glacier, where a local expert will take you on a guided two-hour glacier walk. Then descending from Norway's highest mountains into its most picturesque fjord country, catch a ferry, cross another staggering mountain pass, and settle into your fjord-side hotel.

DAY 15   While Norway has towering mountains, her greatest claim to scenic fame is her deep and lush fjords. To get intimate with the best, Sognefjord, do what is often called "Norway in a Nutshell." A fjord cruise will take you into towering narrow canyons, past isolated farms and villages steeped in the mist of waterfalls, and finally to Gudvangen where the road winds up and over more scenic mountain country to Bergen.

DAY 16   Bergen has a rugged charm. Norway's capital long before Oslo, she wears her rich Hanseatic heritage proudly. Enjoy her salty market, stroll the small easy-on-foot old quarter, and ride the lift up a little mountain right downtown for a commanding city view. After a busy Bergen day, treat yourself to a grand Norwegian-style smorgasbord dinner.

DAY 17   Rounding the corner and beginning the return to Copenhagen, drive along the Hardanger fjord or island-hop south from Bergen to get a feel for Norway's rugged Atlantic coast before heading inland and finally up and over a mountain pass into the remote—and therefore very traditional—Setesdal valley.

DAY 18   Today is easy, with plenty of time for this cultural Easter egg hunt called Setesdal. Probably Norway's most traditional cranny, this valley is a mellow montage of derelict farmhouses, sod-roofed water mills, gold and silver smiths in action, ancient churches, yellowed recipes, rivers, forests, and mountains. You'll spend the evening in Kristiansand, the closest thing Norway has to a beach resort town, and then sail through the night to Denmark.

DAY 19   Good morning, you're back in Denmark! Sand dunes, Lego toys, fortified old towns, and moated manor houses, this is Jutland and it's far from Copenhagen. Spend the morning in the wonderfully preserved old town of Arhus, Jutland's capital and Denmark's second largest city. By evening, after a long drive, nestle into the quiet and quaint island of Aero.

DAY 20   The sleepy isle of Aero is the perfect time-passed world to wind down, enjoy the seagulls, and take a bike ride. Today is yours. Pedal a rented bike into the essence of Denmark. Lunch in a traditional "Kro" country inn. Settle in a cobbled world of sailors who, after someone connected a steam engine to a propeller, decided, "Maybe building ships in bottles is more my style."

DAY 21   For a grand finale and one last flurry of exciting sightseeing activity as you return to Copenhagen, spend the morning in Odense, the home of Hans Christian Andersen and a fine open-air folk museum. After lunch on one last ferry ride, visit Roskilde, with its great Viking ships and royal cathedral, before returning to that wonderful city of Copenhagen.

DAY 22   Today your tour is over. The circle is complete and you've experienced the best 22 days Norway, Sweden, and Denmark have to offer. Of course there's lots more to see and next year you may want 22 more days. But for now, go home, rest up, get your pictures developed, and let your next travel dream off its leash.

Itinerary Options
Actually, with days 1 and 22 your arrival and departure days, this is a skimpy 22-day plan. If you have another day, use it at day 14 (Norway's mountains, glaciers, and fjords) and day 19 (Arhus and Jutland in Denmark), when my suggested itinerary is most rushed. I'd keep things loose, and if the weather's good on Norway's west coast, take an extra day to do the day 14 sights more thoroughly. With disappointing weather, spend the day in and around Arhus on the way to Aero.

Also, as explained in the text, the stretch from Bergen to Aero is meager thrills per mile. You could streamline your trip by arranging an open-jaws plan, starting in Copenhagen (doing day 20, Aero, as a side trip from there) and flying home from Bergen.

BACK DOOR TRAVEL PHILOSOPHY
AS TAUGHT IN *EUROPE THROUGH THE BACK DOOR*

Travel is intensified living—maximum thrills per minute and one of the last great legal sources of adventure. In many ways, the less you spend, the more you get.

Experiencing the real thing requires candid informality— going "Through the Back Door."

Affording travel is a matter of priorities. Many people who "can't afford a trip" could sell their car and travel for two years.

You can travel anywhere in the world for $40 a day plus transportation costs. Money has little to do with enjoying your trip. In fact, spending more money builds a thicker wall between you and what you came to see.

A tight budget forces you to travel "close to the ground," meeting and communicating with the people, not relying on service with a purchased smile. Never sacrifice sleep, nutrition, safety, or cleanliness in the name of budget. Simply enjoy the local-style alternatives to expensive hotels and restaurants.

Extroverts have more fun. If your trip is low on magic moments, kick yourself and start making things happen.

If you don't enjoy a place, it's often because you don't know enough about it. Seek the truth. Recognize tourist traps.

A culture is legitimized by its existence. Give a people the benefit of your open mind. Think of things as different but not better or worse.

Of course, travel, like the world, is a series of hills and valleys. Be fanatically positive and militantly optimistic.

Travel is addicting. It can make you a happier American as well as a citizen of the world. Our Earth is home to five billion equally important people. It's wonderfully humbling to travel and find that people don't envy Americans. They like us, but with all due respect, they wouldn't trade places.

Globe-trotting destroys ethnocentricity and encourages the understanding and appreciation of various cultures. Travel changes people. Many travelers toss aside their "hometown blinders," assimilating the best points of different cultures into their own character.

The world is a cultural garden. We're tossing the ultimate salad. Raise your travel dreams to their upright and locked position and join us.

ARRIVE IN COPENHAGEN

Start your Scandinavian adventure in Copenhagen, the most direct and least expensive place to fly into from the U.S.A. and the gateway to Scandinavia from points south in Europe.

Depart from the U.S.A., and land at Copenhagen's Kastrup Airport the next day. Bus downtown, get set up in hotel or room, and visit the tourist office (possibly en route to hotel) to check plans and pick up information on Copenhagen and Denmark. Then take the "Copenhagen's Heart and Soul" orientation walk described below.

Arrival at Kastrup Airport

If any airport tries harder to make your entry smooth and stress-free, it's Copenhagen's Kastrup Airport. People pop out into Denmark marveling at its efficiency. You'll find a lavish duty-free shopping mall, a grocery store, bakery, cheap booze (for departing passengers only), and a tourist information desk. English is spoken everywhere. Do your banking here: the rates are fine and the steep 35 kr fee for changing checks is standard. (Change plenty to avoid further fees. Get a pile of 1 kr coins for telephoning.) Visit the tourist info desk. Pick up a city map, "This

Week in Copenhagen," and if you're buying the "Copenhagen Card," do so now since it covers your bus trip into
town. Save a few minutes by doing your TI and bank work
while you wait for your luggage.

By the way, most U.S.A.-Copenhagen flights (SAS, TWA,
and Northwest Orient) arrive between 8:00 and 12:00 and
depart from 12:00 to 14:00.

Cheap Tricks: Get used to stretching lunch out of breakfast. SAS serves easy-to-pack rolls and cheese (have zip-
lock in day bag, will travel). Also, their in-flight magazine
has a good little Scandinavia map you may want to "rip
off." If you need to kill a night at the airport, it has wonderful budget "rest cabins" or Hvilekabiner (cheap singles
or doubles with showers, rented by the eight-hour
period, tel. 31 50 93 33, extension 2455).

Getting Downtown: Taxis are fast and easy but fairly
expensive (100 kr to town center). The SAS shuttle buses
will zip you downtown in 20 minutes for 25 kr. City bus
#32 gets you downtown (city hall square, TI) in 40
minutes for only 12 kr (leaves four times an hour, across
the street and to the right 300 yards from the airport). If
you're going to my recommended rooms in Christianshavn, ride #32 to Sundbyvester Place and change (free)
to #2 to Christianshavn Torv.

Setting Up: If you haven't already reserved a room,
find a phone booth at the airport and let your fingers do
the walking with the places listed below or call "Use It"
for a private room (free service, see below). With the city
map, the excellent bus system, and so many friendly
English-speaking Danes, you should have no trouble. If
you've already got your car that's too bad. Find a good
place to park it and leave it there until Day 4.

Copenhagen (Kobenhavn)

Copenhagen is huge—with 1½ million people, a quarter
of all Danes, it's Scandinavia's largest city—but the visitor
rarely leaves the compact old town and can do nearly
everything on foot. The medieval walls that once circled
this old center are now roads: Vestervoldgade (literally,

western wall street), Norrevoldgade, and Ostervoldgade.
The fourth side is the harbor and the island of Slotshol-
men where "Koben" (merchants) "havn" (harbor) was
born in 1167. The next of the city's islands is Amager,
where you'll find the local "Little Amsterdam" district of
Christianshavn—a never-a-dull-moment hodge-podge
of chic, artistic, hippie and hobo. The former moat is now
a string of pleasant lakes and parks, including Tivoli
Gardens. To the north is the old "new town" where the
Amalienborg Palace is surrounded by streets on a grid
plan and the "Little Mermaid" poses relentlessly, waiting
for her sailor to return and the tourists to leave.

It's a great walking town, bubbling with street life and
colorful pedestrian zones. The place is superorganized
for visitors, and on a sunny day you'll very likely find
yourself singing, "Wonderful wonderful Copenhagen."

Tourist Information
Coping with Copenhagen is easy if you take advantage of
the local tourist services. The central tourist office, in the
wax museum building facing the city hall (a short walk
around the Tivoli park from the train station at H. C.
Andersen's Boulevard 22, tel. 33 11 13 25, open daily
June-September 9:00-18:00; October-May 9:00-17:00;
Saturday 9:00-12:00; closed Sunday), is very helpful. Pick
up brochures on Copenhagen (map, "This Week,"
"Copenhagen on Foot") and for all of Denmark (for this
tour: Aero, Roskilde, Odense, Frederiksborg Castle, Louisiana Museum, Arhus, Legoland, and ferry schedules).
Confirm your sightseeing plans for the next three days
and ask about any special events.

"Copenhagen This Week" is a free, handy, and mis-
named monthly guide to the city. It's worth reading for
its good maps, up-to-the-minute list of museum hours,
and calendar of special events. Know that book and use it.

Hovedbanegarden (the main train station) has an efficient room-finding service (Vaerelseanvisning, tel. 33 12
40 45 or 33 12 28 80) that can nearly always find you a
bed. Open daily from 9:00 to 24:00, they have a long list

of private rooms mostly 10 to 15 minutes by bus from the center with doubles for under 200 kr. Their hotels are much more expensive (500 kr dbls). Off-season, shorter hours and closed Sundays.

Also in the main station you'll find a post office, modern telecommunication center, grocery store (open 8:00-24:00 daily), and the Interail Center. The Interail Center is a service the station offers to young travelers. Your Youth Eurailpass, BIGE, Transalpino ticket, or Interail pass is your ticket to a very pleasant lounge, 10 kr showers, free (if risky) luggage storage, maps, snacks, information, and other young travelers. Open June-September, 6:30-24:00. Take advantage of it, unless you're too old.

"Use It" is another great service. This "branch" of Huset, a hip government-sponsored, student-run cluster of cafes, theaters, and galleries, caters to Copenhagen's young but welcomes travelers of any age. It's a friendly and energetic no-nonsense source of budget travel information, with a free room-finding service, ride-finding board, cheap transportation deals, free luggage storage, lockers, and good maps. Brochures explain self-guided tours for bikers, walkers, and those riding scenic bus #6. They have their own list of private rooms, cheaper (150-200 kr doubles) and just as good as the station's. Just plain very helpful. Open daily 9:00-19:00 mid-June to mid-September; Monday-Friday 10:00-16:00 the rest of the year. "Use It" is ten-minute walk from the station at Radhustraede 13, tel. 33 15 65 18. After hours, their night board lists the cheapest rooms available in town.

The Copenhagen Card covers nearly all public transportation and admissions to sights in greater Copenhagen, which stretches from Helsingor to Roskilde. It covers virtually all the city sights, Tivoli, and the bus in from the airport. Available at any tourist office (including the airport's) and the central station: 1 day—105 kr, 2 days—170 kr, 3 days—215 kr. With our plan, this card is probably not worth buying, but check it out yourself.

Confirm anything questionable. Phone booths are everywhere, calls are cheap (1 kr), everyone speaks English, "This Week" and this book list phone numbers for

everything you'll be doing. (Note: All telephone calls in
Denmark, even local ones, must include eight digits.
There are no more area codes.)

Transportation in Copenhagen

While Copenhagen is a great walking town, don't hesitate
to take advantage of its fine bus (information tel. 31 95 17
01) and subway system called "S-tog" (Eurail valid on S-
tog). A joint fare system covers greater Copenhagen. You
pay 8 kr as you board for an hour's travel within two
zones or buy a yellow "klipkort" giving you 10 rides for
70 kr from the driver. Bus drivers are patient and speak
English. City maps list bus and subway routes clearly.
Locals are friendly and will help a lost traveler with a gracious smile. Taxis are plentiful and easy to flag down. (A
five-minute ride, from Rosenborg Castle to Christiansborg Castle, for instance, costs 30 kr.) Four people often
travel cheaper by taxi than by bus.

Pedaling through Copenhagen on a rental bike is a
great way to enjoy the town. The roads are biker-friendly,
and "Use It" has a great biking guide brochure. Rent bikes
at: Central Station Reventlowsgade (tel. 33 14 07 17, daily
7:00-19:00, Saturday 9:00-15:00, closed Sunday) and Dan
Wheel (3 Colbjornsensgade, on the corner of Vesterbrogade, open 9:00-17:30, Saturday and Sunday 9:00-
14:00, 40 kr per day, 60 kr for 2 days, tel. 31 21 22 27). Ask
about the new "Bycykel" program for free bike rental
from the City Hall Square or Central Station.

Planning Ahead

Now's the time to lay the groundwork for a smooth trip.
Any travel agent can book your Stockholm-Helsinki-
Stockholm and Kristiansand-Hirtshals boat rides (push
for special discounts). Any hotels or rooms you know
you want should be reserved by telephone now if you
know for certain when you'll be there and don't think
you'll need lots of flexibility. Reserve your last night in
Copenhagen now. And call in a reservation for the
Denmark-Sweden ferry.

Denmark, Norway, and Sweden all have national tourist

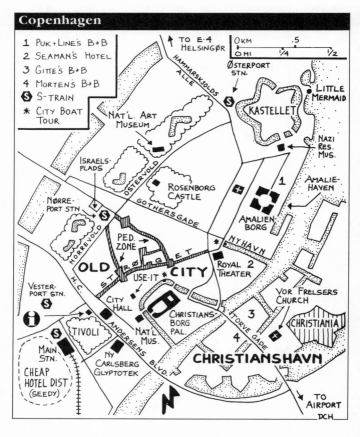

Copenhagen

1 PUK + LINE'S B + B
2 SEAMAN'S HOTEL
3 GITTE'S B + B
4 MORTEN'S B + B
🇸 S-TRAIN
✳ CITY BOAT TOUR

TO E·4 HELSINGØR

0 KM   ·5
0 MI   ¼   ½

ØSTERPORT STN.

LITTLE MERMAID

KASTELLET

NAT'L. ART MUSEUM

NAZI RES. MUS.

ISRAELS-PLADS

ROSENBORG CASTLE

AMALIE-HAVEN

NØRRE-PORT STN

GOTHERSGADE

AMALIEN-BORG

1

NØRREVOLD

ØSTERVOLD

PED. ZONE

NYHAVN

OLD   CITY

USE·IT

ROYAL THEATER

2

VESTER-PORT STN.

H.C.

VOR FRELSERS CHURCH

3

CITY HALL

CHRISTIANIA

CHRISTIANS-BORG PAL.

TIVOLI

NAT'L MUS.

ANDERSENS BLVD.

TORVE GADE

4

MAIN STN.

NY CARLSBERG GLYPTOTEK

CHRISTIANSHAVN

CHEAP HOTEL DIST (SEEDY)

TO AIRPORT

DCH

offices in Copenhagen where you can pick up maps and brochures covering each of your planned stops. The Scandinavian countries are generous with their tourist propaganda. Denmark's is at the city office (facing city hall, see above), Sweden's is just across from the station at Vester Farimags Gate 1 (tel. 01 12 61 06, open Monday-Friday 10:00-15:00, those driving be sure to pick up a Stockholm map), and Norway's is out by the mermaid on Trondhjems Plads (tel. 31 38 41 47, open Monday-Friday 10:00-12:00 and 13:00-15:00).

First Day Orientation Walk: "Copenhagen's Heart and Soul"

After you're set up for the night, set out and get to know the lay of the land. This walk provides a good orientation and is a pleasant way to keep your jet-laggy body moving until a reasonable European bedtime. (Remember, jet-lag hates exercise, fresh air, bright light, and broccoli.) Whenever you run out of steam, just catch a bus or taxi back to your room.

Start from Radhuspladsen (City Hall Square), the bustling heart of Copenhagen, dominated by the spire of the City Hall. On a pedestal left of the City Hall, note the "Lur-Blowers" sculpture. The lur is a horn used over 3,000 years ago. You can see the ancient originals (which still play) in the National Museum and on most tiny butter tubs. Over by the less ancient Burger King, you'll see Copenhagen's main—and Europe's first—pedestrian street, Stroget. Stroget (pron. stroy-et) is actually a series of colorful streets and lively squares that bunny hop right through the old town, connecting the City Hall Square with Kongens Nytorv (The Kings New Square, a 15-minute walk away), where you'll find the Royal Theater and Nyhavn, a recently gentrified sailors' quarter. This formerly sleazy harbor is an interesting mix of tattoo parlors, taverns, and trendy (mostly expensive) cafes lining a canal filled with glamorous old sailboats of all sizes. Any historic sloop is welcome to moor here in Copenhagen's ever-changing boat museum.

Continuing north, along the harborside, you'll pass a huge ship that sails to Oslo every evening. Follow the water to the modern fountain of Amaliehaven Park. The nearby Amalienborg Palace and Square is a good example of orderly baroque planning. Queen Margrethe II and her family live in the palace to your immediate left as you enter the square from the harbor side. Her son and heir to the throne, Frederik, recently moved into the palace directly opposite his mother's. While the guards change at noon (only when Queen is in residence), they shower every morning.

Leave the square on Amaliegade, heading north to Kastellet (Citadel) Park and a small museum about Denmark's World War II resistance efforts. A short stroll past the Gefion fountain and a church made of flint and along the water brings you to the overrated and overphotographed symbol of Copenhagen—the Little Mermaid.

You can get back downtown on foot, by taxi, or on buses #1 or #9 from the other side of Kastellet Park (a special bus runs from the mermaid in summer).

Accommodations
Hotels
By far the expensive option in a costly city with plenty of fine alternatives, hotels will generally run you over US$100 (625 kr) per double. Here are your best decent budget choices in the center (with doubles for $60 to $100 with breakfast).

Near Norreport S-tog stop (a great locale near the ped zone and station): **Ibsen's Hotel** is a rare simple, bath down the hall, cheery, very clean and central budget hotel, just two blocks from the Norreport Station. This is the best cheap hotel in town, with a management that treats you like you're paying top dollar. They'll hold a room with a phone call (500 kr doubles including breakfast, Vendersgade 23, DK 1363, tel. 33 13 19 13).

Jorgensens Hotel is the cheapest hotel in town with 250 kr doubles without breakfast. In the summer, beds are rented in small dorms for 100 kr each (nearly always available). This place is popular (only) with young and gay travelers (Romersgade 11, tel. 33 13 97 43).

Hotel KFUM Soldaterhjem, originally for soldiers, is on the fifth floor with no elevators, and with unreliable reception hours, so call first (300 kr without breakfast, Gothersgade 115, Copenhagen K, tel. 33 15 40 44).

Near the station: Behind the station on the edge of drugs, porno, and prostidumpiness are several handy, friendly, safe-on-the-inside, and decent hotels. The older, more traditional, stately but well worn **Missionshotellet Nebo** is my choice here (doubles for 715 kr with buffet breakfast and shower, 485 kr without shower, Istedgade 6, tel. 31 21 12 17).

Near Nyhavn: Sofolkenes Mindehotel, a retired seaman's hotel, is the cheapest real hotel in town. It's in a great, quiet, central location, one block off Nyhavn. The management is friendly. Rooms are small, a bit dingy, but functional; the cafeteria is cheap. Doubles cost 400 kr with breakfast, lots of singles for 220 kr. Triples and quads cost less per person (Peder Skrams Gade 19, D-1054, tel. 33 13 48 82).

Other inexpensive downtown Copenhagen hotels worth considering are **Hotel Sankt Jorgen** (450 kr dbls, Julius Thomsensgade 22, DK-1632 Copenhagen V, tel. 31 37 15 11) and **Hotel 9 Sma Hjem** (450 kr dbls, Classensgade 40, DK-2100 Copenhagen O, tel. 31 26 16 47).

Youth Hostels

Copenhagen accommodates the young vagabond on a shoestring very nicely. The "Use It" office is your best source of information. Each of these places charges 70 to 100 kr per person for bed and breakfast. If you don't have your own hostel sheet, you'll normally have to rent one for around 25 kr. IYHF hostels require a membership card.

The **Copenhagen Hostel** (IYHF) is very modern, with doubles and quints only, no curfew, excellent facilities, cheap meals, laundry, efficiently managed, on the edge of town, bus #46 from the station (Sjaellandsbroen 55, 2300 Copenhagen S, tel. 32 52 29 08).

The **Bellahoj Hostel** (IYHF) is large, impersonal, in a park setting with 8 to 12 beds per room, 20 minutes from the station on bus #2 (Herbergvejen 8, 2700 Bronshoj, tel. 31 28 97 15).

KFUK/KFUM (Danish YMCA/YWCA) has a great location in the pedestrian center but musty and depressing rooms (Kannikestraede 19 on Grabrodretorv just off Stroget, tel. 33 11 30 31, closed 10:00-15:00 daily). There's a similar one at Valdersgade 15 (tel. 31 31 15 74).

The **Sleep-In** (Per Henrik Lings Alle 6, tel. 31 26 50 59, late June through August, 4-bed cubicles in a huge coed room, no curfew, pretty wild, usually has room) is popular with the desperate or adventurous. Sleeping bag required. No curfew. Free rubbers.

Hippies feel welcome and sleep free at **Christiania**.

Private Rooms

Each Copenhagen room-finding service cultivates its own list of people who rent rooms to travelers. Here are a few leads for Copenhagen's best accommodation values. By booking direct, you'll save yourself and your host the tourist office's fee. Always call ahead. Each family speaks English and will hold your room until 17:00. For long distance reservations, follow this procedure: (1) telephone from the U.S.A. (it only costs $1 a minute) to check on availability and price and to make the preliminary reservation, (2) follow up with a letter explaining what you figure you've reserved and requesting written confirmation, (3) your host will confirm with a return letter. If, for whatever reason, you need to cancel, it's no problem, just let your host know. They wait and worry otherwise.

In Christianhavn: This area is artsy, colorful, and residential, with street people, lots of shops, cafes, and canals, a ten-minute walk to the center, and with good bus connections to the airport and downtown. **Gitte Kongstad**, a fun, colorful schoolteacher thoroughly enjoys sharing her restored 1782 warehouse-turned-penthouse with my readers. You'll feel at home as soon as Gitte greets you at the door (single—175 kr, double—225 kr, triple—300 kr, great breakfast worth Gitte's 35 kr extra charge, 4th floor with no elevator, TVs in each room, at Skt. Annaegade 1 B, 4 tv., 1416 Copenhagen K, tel. 31 57 24 66). Take bus #32, then #2 from airport, bus #8 or #2 from the station or City Hall, just over Knippels Bridge on corner of Strandgade and St. Annaegade. If Gitte's full, she nearly always has a friend with a room for you nearby.

Morten Frederiksen, A very laid-back ponytailed sort of guy, runs this mod-funky-pleasant loft. It's a clean, comfy, good look at today's hip Danish life-style, and has a great location right on Christianshavn's main drag (only 150 kr for a double, 2 minutes from Gitte's at Torvegade 36, tel. 31 95 32 73).

Near the Amalienborg Palace: This is a stately embassy neighborhood—no stress but a bit bland. Very safe, and you can look out your window to see the queen's place (and the guards changing), a ten-minute walk north of Nyhavn and Stroget. **Line Voutsinos** (Amaliegade 34, 3rd floor, tel. 33 14 71 42) and her friend **Puk La Cour** (pron. "pook"; Amaliegade 34, 4th floor, tel. 33 12 04 68) are both young, professional, mod, bright, cheery, open, and easygoing women who keep busy with their families but love having guests. They charge 200 kr per double, less per person in a triple or quad.

In another area, a ten-minute walk from the station, friendly **Maria Gad** speaks just a little English and rents one small room (120 kr for single, 175 kr as a double) in her bright, cheery apartment (just past the lake called Skt. Jorgens So., Vodroffsveg 29, fifth floor [elevator], tel. 31 31 24 81).

Food

Copenhagen's many good restaurants are well listed by category in the "This Week" publication. Since restaurant prices include 22% tax and 15% service, your budget may require alternatives. These survival tips for the hungry budget traveler in Copenhagen are worth noting:

Picnic: Irma and Brugsen are the two largest supermarket chains. Netto and Aldi are cut-rate outfits with the cheapest prices. The little grocery store in the central station (open daily from 8:00 to 24:00) is great for picnic stuff. You'll find a delightful outdoor fruit and vegetable market at Israels Plads.

Viktualiehandler (small delis) and bakeries, found on nearly every corner, sell fresh bread, tasty pastries, juice, milk, cheese, and yogurt (tall liter boxes, drinkable). Liver paste is cheap and good.

Smorrebrod: Denmark's famous open face sandwiches

cost a fortune in restaurants, but the many smorrebrod shops sell them for 6 to 22 kr. Drop into one of these often no-name, family run, open 11:00-15:00 budget-savers, and get several elegant OFS's to go. The tradition calls for three sandwich courses: herring first, then meat, then cheese. It makes for a classy—and cheap—picnic. Downtown you'll find these handy local alternatives to Yankee fast food chains: Centrum at 6 C. Vesterbrogade (long hours, across from station and Tivoli), Smorrebrods Forretningen at 28 Gronnegade (8:00-14:00, closed Saturday and Sunday, near Kongens Nytorv), Domhusets Smorrebrod at 18 Kattesundet (7:00-14:30), Sorgenfri just off the Stroget at 8 Brolaeggerstraede (Monday-Friday 11:00-14:00) and one at the corner of Magstraede and Radhusstraede (Monday-Friday, 8:00-14:30, next to "Husit/Use It"). In Christianshavn, Franske Kokken is on Torvegade near Wildersgade. And in Nyhavn, a good sandwich shop is on the corner of Holbergsgade and Peder Skram Gade.

The "Polse": The famous Danish hot dog, sold in "polsevognen" (sausage wagons) throughout the city, is one of the few typically Danish institutions to resist the onslaught of our global fast food culture. They are fast, cheap, tasty, easy to order ("hot dog" is a Danish word for weenie, study the photo menu for variations), and almost worthless nutritionally. Still the local "dead man's finger" is the dog kids love to bite.

By hanging around a polsevognen you can study this institution. It's a form of social care: only difficult-to-employ people, such as the handicapped, are licensed to run these wienermobiles. As they gain seniority they are promoted to more central locations. Danes gather here for munchies and "polsesnak" (sausage talk), the local slang for empty chatter.

Cheap Restaurants: Cafeterias (in department stores, especially top floor of Illums, an elegant circus of reasonable food under a glass dome, Magasin, or Daell's Varehus at Norregade 12, at the Sofolkenes Mindehotel, in the "Use It" complex, at the University Cafe—Fiolstraede 2), fast food joints (everywhere), and pizzerias (look for salad bars and all-you-can-eat specials) offer Copenhagen's cheapest sit-down meals. Pasta Basta (Valkensdorf 22 near Grabrodretorv, cheap all-you-can-eat special, open late) is very popular and just off Stroget. Alexander's Pizza Bar serves all the pizza and salad you can stand for 70 kr (just off Stroget near University at Lille Kannikestr 5).

Koltbord is the Danish word for smorgasbord (an all-you-can-eat buffet). This is a fine and fun budget way to explore your way through a world of traditional Danish food. The best and handiest is the famous "Koldtbord" at the central station's Bistro Restaurant. Its 50 kr breakfast is served from 7:00 to 10:00 and the 115 kr dinner is from 11:00 to 21:30 daily. You'll enjoy a great variety. Study the menu options. Tel. 33 14 12 32.

Good Eating in Christianshavn: Just around the corner from Gitte's B&B you can enjoy good 75 kr "dagens ret" meals with a trendy but very local crowd at **Cafe Wilder** or **Luna Cafe**. Locals also love the **La Novo** Italian restaurant at Torvegade 49 where the 50 kr lasagna is a meal in itself. The **Franske Kokken** (Torvegatan near the bridge), serves take-out sandwiches. Right on the community square you'll find a grocery store, fruit stands under the Greenlanders monument, and a bakery (at the bus stop, Torvegade 45). The **Ravelin Restaurant** (Torvegatan 79) serves good traditional Danish-style food at reasonable prices to happy local crowds on a lovely lakeside terrace (only on sunny days).

Eating Downtown: Parnas (live piano sing-song nearly nightly at 21:30, Lille Kongensgade 4, tel. 33 12 12 24) and Skindbuksen (Lille Kongensgade 4, tel. 33 12 90 37) are both cozy, atmospheric, dark, reasonable, popular with locals, and just off Stroget. Vin and Olgod (Skindergade 45, 20:00-02:00, closed Sundays, tel. 33 13 26 25) is the place to go for old-time sing, dance, eat, and drink rowdiness.

DAYS 2 and 3
COPENHAGEN

You'll feel right at home in Scandinavia's largest (and most loved) city after a busy day of sightseeing, including a look at the royal palace, city views from a dizzy church spire, a relaxing canal boat ride, and a special look at Copenhagen through the eyes of a local historian who'll walk you right into the city's colorful past.

Suggested Schedule Day 2	
8:00	Your first of many huge Scandinavian breakfasts.
9:00	Browse around Christianshavn, Copenhagen's "little Amsterdam," climb the unique outside spiral staircase of Our Savior's church (Vor Frelsers), and buy a picnic lunch.
10:00	Walk over to the Christiansborg Palace. Catch the 10:00 free 30-minute tour of the Parliament and/or explore the subterranean Christiansborg Castle ruins under today's palace.
11:00	Take a guided tour of Denmark's royal Christiansborg Palace.
12:00	Catch the harbor tour boat, a relaxing overview of the city's harbors, a trip out to the famous mermaid, and a good time to munch your picnic.
13:00	Free afternoon to shop and stroll the Stroget pedestrian mall.
15:00	Tour the Rosenborg Castle and crown jewels. Siesta in the park.
17:30	Meet Helge "Jack" Jacobsen for a city walking tour (16:30 on Sunday).
20:00	All-you-can-eat Danish smorgasbord at the station's Bistro restaurant.
21:30	Spend the evening in Tivoli Gardens.

Suggested Schedule Day 3	
10:00	Trace Denmark's cultural roots in the National Museum.
12:00	Ny Carlsberg Glyptotek art gallery.
13:00	Smorrebrod lunch.
14:00	Free afternoon with many options, including: Carlsberg Brewery tour, the Nazi Resistance Museum and Amalienborg Palace square, more shopping and browsing, another Jack Jacobsen walking tour (each day is different).
Evening	Feel the pulse of Scandinavia's most fun-loving city with the help of listings in "Copenhagen This Week," the more hip "Use It Playtime" guide or your B&B hostess's advice.

Savor Copenhagen's two claims to fame, spending an afternoon on Europe's greatest pedestrian shopping street and the evening in the Continent's first and ultimate amusement park, the famous Tivoli Gardens.

Wonderful Copenhagen requires a very busy second day. The National Museum is a must. After that, choose among a brewery tour (with free samples), great art including Rodin's "Thinker," a peek at Denmark's impressive World War II Nazi resistance movement, browsing through shops that specialize in Danish design, a look at the crown jewels at the Rosenborg castle, or more shopping. Whatever you do, you'll work up an appetite to justify the eternal buffet "koltbord" dinner at the ever-popular station Bistro restaurant.

Sightseeing Highlights
▲ Copenhagen's Town Hall (Radhus)—This city landmark, between the station/Tivoli/TI and Stroget pedestrian mall, offers private tours and trips up its 350-foot-high tower (30-minute 10 kr tours at 11:00 and 14:00 Monday-Friday, tel. 33 15 38 00).

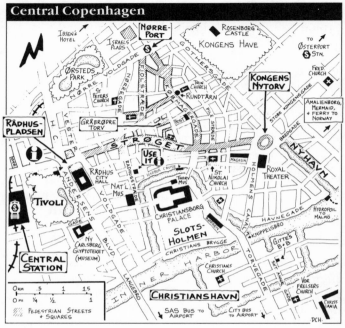

▲**Christiansborg Palace**—This modern "slot" or palace, built on the ruins of the original twelfth-century palace, houses the parliament, supreme court, prime minister's headquarters, and royal reception rooms. Guided 40-minute tours of the reception rooms (in English May-September, Tuesday-Sunday at 11:00, 13:00, 15:00, offseason tours at 11:00 and 13:00 except Monday and Saturday, tel. 33 92 64 92) cost 22 kr. You'll slip-slide on protect-the-floor slippers through 22 rooms and gain a good feel for Danish history, royalty, and politics in this 100-year-old, still-functioning palace. There are also guided tours of the connected Danish Parliament (30 min. long, in Danish, June-September daily on the hour, 10:00-16:00, except Saturday, free, tel. 33 33 37 55 00).

▲**Christiansborg Castle Ruins**—A fine exhibit in the scant remains of the first castle built by Bishop Absalon—the twelfth-century founder of Copenhagen—lies under the palace. (Open daily 9:30-15:30, closed Saturdays in off-season, 11 kr, good 1 kr guide, note it opens 30 minutes before other nearby sights).

▲▲▲ **National Museum**—Focus on the excellent Danish collection, which traces this civilization from its ancient beginnings, laid out on the ground floor chronologically with English explanations. Highlights include passage graves, mummified bodies, the 2,000-year-old Gunderstrup Cauldron, original ancient lur horns, Viking gear, mead drinking horns, and early Christian art. Good English brochures. This free museum is curiously enjoyable. (Open in summer, Tuesday-Sunday 10:00-16:00; off-season, Tuesday-Friday 11:00-15:00, Saturday and Sunday 12:00-16:00, tel. 33 13 44 11).

▲ **Ny Carlsberg Glyptotek**—Scandinavia's top art gallery, with an especially intoxicating Egyptian, Greek, and Etruscan collection and a heady if small exhibit of French nineteenth-century paintings (Gericault, Delacroix, Manet, impressionists, Gauguin before and after Tahiti) is an impressive example of what beer money can do. Linger under the palm leaves and glass dome of the very soothing conservatory. One of the original Rodin "Thinkers" can be seen for free, pondering the garden in the museum's backyard. (Just behind Tivoli, open Tuesday-Sunday 10:00-16:00, 12:00-15:00 off-season, 15 kr, tel. 33 91 10 65.) This is particularly important if you've not seen the great galleries of central Europe.

▲▲▲ **Tivoli Gardens**—The world's most famous amusement park is now 175 years old. It is 20 acres, 110,000 lanterns, and countless ice cream cones of fun. You pay one 28 kr admission price and find yourself lost in a Hans Christian Andersen wonderland of rides, restaurants, games, marching bands, roulette wheels, and funny mirrors. Tivoli is wonderfully Danish. It doesn't try to be Disney. It's open from 10:00 to 24:00, late April through mid-September (closed off-season). Go at night on a full stomach or with a discreet picnic (the food inside is costly). If you must eat inside, there are cheap Polser stands. The Yugoslavian restaurant, Hercegovina, is a decent value (150 kr buffet).

Pick up a map and schedule as you enter and locate a

billboard schedule of events (look for the British flag for
English). Free concerts, mime, ballet, acrobats, puppets,
and other shows pop up all over the park and a well-
organized visitor can enjoy an exciting evening of entertainment without spending a single krone. Rides are reasonable, but the all-day pass for 115 kr is probably best
for those who may have been whirling dervishes in a
previous life. On Wednesday, Friday, Saturday, and Sunday the place closes down (23:45) with a fireworks show.
If you're taking an overnight train out of Copenhagen,
Tivoli—just across from the station—is the best place to
spend your last Copenhagen hours. Tel. 33 15 10 01.

▲▲**Rosenborg Castle**—This impressively furnished
Renaissance-style castle houses the Danish crown jewels
and royal knickknacks. It's musty with history. Pick up
and follow the 1 kr guide page. The castle is surrounded
by the royal gardens, rare plant collection and, on sunny
days, a minefield of sunbathing Danish beauties. (Open
daily 10:00-16:00 in summer, 11:00-15:00 spring and fall,
closed November-March, 30 kr, tel. 33 15 32 86.) There is
a changing of the guard mini-parade from Rosenborg
Castle at 11:30 to Amalienborg Castle at 12:00 when the
queen is in residence.

▲**Denmark's Fight for Freedom Museum (Friheds-
museet)**—The fascinating story of a heroic Nazi resistance struggle is well explained in English. (Between the
Queen's Palace and the Mermaid, daily May to mid-
September, 10:00-16:00 except Mondays, off-season
11:00-15:00, free, tel. 33 13 77 14.)

▲▲▲**"Stroget"**—Copenhagen's experimental 25-year-
old, tremendously successful, and most copied pedestrian shopping mall—a string of serendipitous streets and
lovely squares from the city hall to Nyhavn. Spend some
time browsing, people-watching, and exploring here and
along adjacent pedestrian-only streets. While Stroget
(silent "g") has become quite hamburgerized, charm lurks
in many adjacent areas, like the nearby Grabrodertorv
(Grey Brothers Square). Note: Stroget is not an actual
street but the popular name for a series of individually

named streets. Many of the best night spots are just off Stroget. The best department stores (Illum's and Magazine, see below) are on Stroget.

▲▲▲**Copenhagen on Foot**—Helge (Jack) Jacobsen is an inspirational local historian (possibly old H. C. Andersen himself reincarnated) who takes small groups on daily walks through different slices of Copenhagen. Pick up his "On Foot in Copenhagen" list of tours at the TI or see his walks in the "This Week" calendar, and take advantage of this best way to fall in love with Copenhagen. Jack charges 25 kr (15 kr if you're under 23, through 1991) for his two-hour walk. He has six different tours, normally leaving at 17:30. (The basic one leaves from the Town Hall square on Monday, Wednesday, and Thursday.) Just show up (the schedule tells where) at any walk you can fit in. Tours go rain or shine. As Jack says, "The weather may be worse tomorrow." (Late June through early September, tel. 31 51 25 90.) By the way, Jack has written a very readable concise history of Denmark in English (100 kr, on sale at the National Museum).

▲▲**Harbor Cruise and Canal Tours**—The 50-minute, 35 kr harbor tour leaves from Gammel Strand near Christiansborg Palace and National Museum every half hour from 10:00 until about 16:30 (later if balmy), May through mid-September. It's a pleasant way to see the overrated mermaid and take a load off those weary sightseeing feet. Dress warm; all the boats are open top. Tel. 33 13 31 05. (Clever vandals like to erase one of the "C's" on the tour sign. Don't be confused.) Boats also leave from Nyhavn.

▲**Vor Frelsers (Our Savior's) Church**—The unique spiral spire that you'll admire from afar can be climbed for a great city view and a good aerial view of the Christiania commune below. It's 311 feet high and, they claim (but I haven't counted), 400 steps. While you're there, the church's bright baroque interior is worth a look. Open daily 9:00-16:30, Sunday 12:00-16:30, closes an hour early in spring and fall, completely closed off-season, 10 kr.

Christiania—This is a unique on-again, off-again social experiment, a counterculture utopia attempt that is, to many, disillusioning. An ultra-human mishmash of 1,000 idealists, anarchists, hippies, dope fiends, and nonmaterialists has established squatters' rights in a former military barracks—follow the beer bottles and guitars down Prinsessgade behind Vor Frelsers' spiral church spire in Christianshavn. This communal cornucopia of dogs, dirt, drugs, and dazed people—or haven of peace, freedom, and no taxes, depending on your perspective—is a political hot potato. No one in the establishment wants it—or has the nerve to mash it. While hard drugs are out, hash and pot are sold and smoked openly. Past the souvenir and hash-vendor entry you'll find a fascinating ramshackle world of moats and ramparts, alternative housing, unappetizing falafel stands, a restaurant (Spiseloppen), handicraft shops, and filth. No photos, not safe at night—and, in some people's opinion, not safe ever.

Carlsberg Brewery Tour—Denmark's two beloved sources of legal intoxicants, Carlsberg and Tuborg, offer free brewery tours and tasting. Carlsberg's tour (Monday-Friday 9:00, 11:00, and 2:30, tel. 31 21 12 21 ext. 1312, bus #6 or #18 to 140 Ny Carlsberg Vej) is most popular. Tuborg is at Strandvejen 54, Hellerup (Monday-Friday 10:00, 12:30, and 14:30; tel. 31 29 33 11, ext. 2212).

Other Sights to Consider: The great Copenhagen train station is a fascinating mesh of Scandimanity and transportation efficiency. Even if you're not a train traveler, check it out. The noontime changing of the guard at the Amalienborg Palace is boring: all they change is places. Copenhagen's colorful flea market (summer Saturdays 8:00-14:00 at Israels Plads) is small but feisty and surprisingly cheap. Nyhavn, with its fine old ships, tattoo shops, and jazz clubs, is a wonderful place to hang out. Normal organized big bus city tours leave from the Town Hall Square (90 minutes to 3 hours, 100-150 kr).

Nightlife
Copenhagen is a cool place for jazz. **De Tre Musketerer** (Nicolaj Plads, tel. 33 12 50 67) offers beer, low cover, a middle-aged crowd, and jazz from 21:30. During the ten-

day jazz fest early each July you'll find music everywhere and plenty of tickets. For good dancing, Woodstock (Vestergade 12, tel. 33 11 20 71, low cover, plays my kind of music from 21:00) is filled with people who stop rapping once the door's open. Get the latest from "This Week" or the more hip "Use It Playtime."

The Danes gather at Copenhagen's other great amusement park, **Bakken**—open March-August, daily until midnight, free, a 30-minute subway trip from downtown.

Shopping

The city's top department stores (Illum at 52 Ostergade, tel. 33 14 40 02, and Magasin at 13 Kongens Nytorv, tel. 33 11 44 33) offer a good, if expensive, look at today's Denmark. Both are on Stroget and have fine cafeterias on their top floors. Shops are open Monday until 17:00, Tuesday through Thursday until 17:30, Friday until 20:00, and Saturday until 14:00. The department stores and the Politiken Bookstore on the Radhus Square have a good selection of maps and English travel guides. If you buy over 600 kr ($100) worth of stuff, you can get the 18% VAT (MOMS in Danish) tax back if you buy from a shop displaying the Danish Tax-Free Shopping emblem. Call 36 72 00 66, see "Copenhagen This Week," or ask a merchant for specifics.

Side Trips from Copenhagen

If you're not going to the cute island of Aero (see Day 20), try to visit Dragor, a similarly cozy ship-in-a-bottle-type port town just a few minutes beyond the Copenhagen airport.

If you're making the mistake of not going to Oslo, at least consider the quickie cruise that leaves daily from Copenhagen (departs 17:00, returns 9:15 two days later; 16 hours sailing each way and 7 hours in Norway's capital). Special packages give you a bed in a double cabin, two fine dinners, and two smorgasbord breakfasts for around $200. Cheaper on Sunday-Thursday departures. Call DFDS Scandinavian Seaways at 33 11 22 55.

NORTH ZEALAND AND INTO SWEDEN

Over jet-lag and ready to hit the road, you'll pick up your rental car and drive north to see Zealand's two top sights—the Frederiksborg castle (Denmark's best) and the renowned Louisiana modern art gallery. Then, after a quick ferry ride to Sweden, drive east for two and a half hours through the forests to Vaxjo.

Suggested Schedule	
9:00	Pick up rental car, drive north to Hillerod.
10:00	Tour Frederiksborg Castle.
12:00	Enjoy a picnic lunch marinated in history under the Kronborg castle or soaked in modern art at the Louisiana art gallery.
14:00	Ferry to Helsingborg, Sweden, and drive east.
18:00	Set up in Vaxjo (or Kalmar).

Transportation

To avoid driving in big cities, especially on my first day behind the wheel, I normally try to pick up my rental car at airports. Unfortunately, Copenhagen's is on the south side of town and we're heading north.

Wherever you pick up your rental car, don't rush the orientation. Study the basics: locate the car manual, know how to change a tire and what kind of gas to use, understand their breakdown policy and how to use the local automobile club membership—if one is included. Ask for advice and rules of the local road, a list of drop-off offices, a second key, any map they can give you, and directions to Helsingor. Before leaving, drive around for five or ten minutes. Try everything. Distinguish emergency flashers from windshield wipers. Find problems before they find you.

I always get a second key made as soon as possible, jot down the license and vital information to store in my

Oresund-Greater Copenhagen

money belt, set up a backseat pantry and a trunk deep-storage box. This will be your home for three weeks. You might as well move in right away.

North Zealand by car: Follow signs for E-4 and Helsingor north out of Copenhagen. The freeway is great and very soon it'll hit you: This is a tiny country. Frederiksborg Castle (not to be confused with the nearby Fredensborg slot or palace) is clearly marked in the pleasant town of Hillerod. The Louisiana Museum is on the coast just south of Helsingor in the town of Humlebaek. While the shortest distance between any two points is the autobahn (E-4 in this case), the "Strand" coastal road (#152) is very pleasant, going by some of Denmark's finest mansions.

Getting to Sweden is easy. Just follow the signs to the "Helsingborg, Sweden" ferry. The freeway takes you right there. Boats leave every 20 minutes. You buy your ticket from the man as you roll on board (about $25 for car and driver). Reservations are advisable (tel. 33 14 88 80).

The 30-minute ferry ride gives you just enough time to enjoy the view of the Elsinore "Hamlet" castle, be impressed by how narrow this very important channel is, and change money. The ferry exchange desk's less than great rate is countered by its very low fee. Change enough to get you well into Sweden. In Helsingborg (Swedish customs are a wave-through), follow signs for E-4 and Stockholm. The road's good, traffic's light, you'll make good time. At Ljungby, road 25 takes you to Vaxjo and Kalmar. It's about a six-hour drive from Copenhagen to Kalmar.

Sightseeing Highlights
▲▲**Frederiksborg Castle**—This grandest castle in Scandinavia is often called the Danish Versailles. Frederiksborg (built from 1602 to 1620) is the castle of Christian IV, Denmark's great builder king. You can almost hear the clackle of royal hoofbeats as you walk over the moat through the stately cobbled courtyard, past the Dutch Renaissance brick facade and into the lavish interior. Much of the castle was reconstructed in 1860 with the normal Victorian flair. The English guidebook is unnecessary as many rooms have a handy English information sheet, and there are plenty of tours on which to freeload. Listen for hymns on the old carillon at the top of each hour. The many historic paintings are a fascinating scrapbook of Danish history. Savor the courtyard. Picnic in the moat park, or enjoy the elegant Slotsherrens Kro cafeteria at the moat's edge. The castle is open daily from 10:00 to 17:00 May-September. Off-season it closes at 15:00 or 16:00. 25 kr entry. Easy parking. From Copenhagen, take the S-train to Hillerod and then enjoy a pleasant 20-minute walk, or catch bus #701 (free with S-tog ticket or Eurailpass) from the station (tel. 42 26 04 39).
▲▲**Louisiana**—Beautifully situated on the coast 20 miles north of Copenhagen, this is Scandinavia's most raved about modern art museum. It's a wholistic place— mixing its art, architecture, and landscape masterfully.

Wander from famous Chagalls and Picassos to more
obscure art. Poets spend days here nourishing their creative souls with new angles, ideas, and perspectives. The
views over one of the busiest passages in the nautical
world are nearly as inspiring as the art. The cafeteria
(indoor/outdoor) is reasonable and welcomes picnickers
who buy a drink. Open daily 10:00 to 17:00, Wednesdays
until 22:00. 40 kr admission (or included in a special
round-trip tour's ticket). Tel. 42 19 07 19. Train from
Copenhagen toward Helsingor, getting off in 36 minutes
at Humlebaek. Then it's a free bus connection or a ten-
minute walk through the woods. From Frederiksborg
there are rare Humlebaek buses, but most will have to
connect via Helsingor.

Helsingor—Often confused with its Swedish sister, Helsingborg, just 2 ½ miles across the channel, Helsingor is a
small pleasant town with a medieval center and lots of
Swedes who come over for lower-priced alcohol. (The
bar scene reminds me of *Gunsmoke*.)

▲**Kronborg Castle (Elsinore)** is famous for its questionable (but profitable) ties to Shakespeare. Most of the
"Hamlet" castle you'll see today, darling of every big bus
tour and travelogue, was built long after Hamlet died, and
Shakespeare never saw the place. There was a castle here
in Hamlet's day, however, and there was a troupe of English actors working here in Shakespeare's time (Shakespeare
may have known them or even been one of them). And
hordes of tourists visit. "To see or not to see?" It's most
impressive from the outside. The Kalmar castle (see Day
5) is a better medieval castle. But you're here, and if you
like castles, see it. (Buy only tickets 1 and 2 for 16 kr.
Don't miss the 20-minute dungeon tours that leave on the
half hour. There are English explanations printed in the
royal apartments, open daily, 10:30-17:00, less off-
season.) The grounds between the walls and sea are free
and great for a picnic with a pleasant view of the busy
strait separating Denmark and Sweden. If you're rushed,
the view from the ferry is as close as you need to get.
There's a fine beachfront hostel (Vandrerhjem Villa
Moltke, tel. 49 21 16 40) just a mile north of the castle. I've

Denmark and Southern Sweden

met people who prefer small towns and small prices touring Copenhagen with this hostel as their base.

Vaxjo—A pleasant, rather dull town of 50,000, Vaxjo is
incredibly hard to pronounce. Try "veck fwah." It's in the
center of Smaland—the Swedish province famous for its
forests, lakes, great glass, and many emigrants to the
U.S.A. A stroll through downtown Vaxjo is as purely a
Swedish experience as I think you can have. The town is
compact, with the train station, town square, two important museums, and the tourist office (Kronobergsgatan 8,
tel. 0470/41410) all within two blocks of each other.

Accommodations in Vaxjo

Hotel Esplanad is your best central hotel value. 410 kr
doubles from mid-June through mid-August, including
breakfast. Too expensive other times. Esplanad 21A, tel.
0470/22580.

 Sara Hotel Statt is very central, more traditional, and
borderline luxurious. Doubles cost 1,000 kr, but the 620

kr weekend and summer rate including breakfast is a
good value. 6 Kungsgatan, tel. 0470/13400.

Kinnevaldsgardens Motel is a homey place run by
Eva and Lasse Andersson (and their three children) like a
British B&B. They have four doubles, 270 kr each, and
are generous with maps, information, and evening cake
and coffee. Breakfast is 20 kr extra. St. Vagen 9, Bergsnas.
(Don't take the blue Vaxjo exit; keep following the green
Vaxjo centrum signs, just outside of town, leave freeway
25 on the "Morners Vag" exit, and turn in the direction of
Ojaby. It's across the street from the Q-8 gas station. Tel.
0470/60887. Bus #4 for 7 kr from the station in Vaxjo.)

The **Bergsnas Motel** just across the street (no character and a bit musty, but cheap: 300 kr doubles) is run by
the friendly man in the Q-8 gas station at Stora Vagen 11,
tel. 0470/60071.

The modern **Scandic** chain hotel has reasonable rooms
on the edge of town (Hejaregatan 19, tel. 0470/22070).

Vaxjo has a fine youth hostel on a lake, 2 ½ miles out of
town. **STF Vandrarhem Evedal (IYHF)**, 35590 Vaxjo,
tel. 0470/63070. Open from 8:00 to 9:30 and 17:00 to
22:00, 2-4 bed rooms, 73 kr (breakfast—38 kr), telephone
reservations required in summer. Take bus #1 or #1B from
the tourist office to the last stop (summer only, last ride
18:15, first ride 10:00 so hitch a ride into Vaxjo with a fellow hosteler).

For a 25 kr fee, the tourist office (9:00-19:00, Saturday
10:00-14:00, Sunday 13:00-16:00) can always find private
rooms for 135 kr per person, 110 kr if you have sheets (tel.
0470/41410).

VAXJO, KALMAR, AND GLASS COUNTRY

Outside of Stockholm, Smaland is the most interesting region of Sweden. More Americans came from here than any part of Scandinavia, and the immigration center in Vaxjo tells the story well. This is "glass country" and several prestigious glassworks welcome curious visitors. Kalmar has a rare Old World ambience and my favorite castle in Scandinavia. The strange island of Oland offers a mixed bag of beaches, bird-watching, Stonehenge-type mysteries, and windmills.

Suggested Schedule	
9:00	Tour Vaxjo, its Smalands folk museum and the impressive Emigrants Center. Drive into glass country.
11:30	Tour a small traditional glassworks (Bergdala) and a big famous modern one (Orrefors).
14:30	Set up in Kalmar in time to see the castle and its new provincial museum (Lansmuseet).
18:00	Enjoy an easy evening in the old town.

Sightseeing Highlights
▲▲ **House of Emigrants**— 1,300,000 Swedes moved to the U.S.A., and most came from this neck of the Swedish woods. If you have roots here, this place is really exciting. If not, it's mildly interesting. The Dream of America exhibit tells the story of the 1850-1920s "American Fever." (The emigration festival, second Sunday in August, is a real hoot as thousands of Minnesotans storm the town.) Upstairs is an excellent library and research center. Rootseekers are very welcome. Advance notice is urged (write well in advance to Box 201, S-351 04, Vaxjo, for research form and information, bring what information you have—like ship names and birthdays). Open Monday-

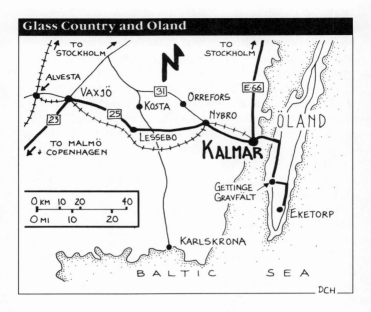

Glass Country and Oland

Friday 9:00-17:00, Saturday 11:00-15:00, Sunday
13:00-17:00, shorter hours off-season, tel. 0470/20120, 20
kr. The research center is open Monday-Friday only, 25
kr. The man at the desk looks frighteningly like the heavy-
set older brother in *The Immigrants* (If you haven't seen
the movie, rent it and its sequel, *The New Land*, and see
them before you leave home).

Smalands Museum—This cute small-townish museum
(one of Sweden's oldest) offers a good look at local for-
estry, a prehistoric exhibit, a wonderful traditional cos-
tume display (top floor) and, most important, an
introduction to the area's glass industry. Nothing is in
English, but there's a helpful and free English brochure.
Monday-Friday 9:00-16:00, Saturday 11:00-15:00, Sunday
13:00-17:00, 10 kr. Oh, go on, see it—it's just next to the
Emigrants House.

Vaxjo also has a fine cathedral, a lovely park with an
arboretum, and a pleasant pedestrian center. The tourist
office, station, and all sights are clustered very close
together.

Lessebo Papermill—You'll pass right through Lessebo
en route to Orrefors (just after the Kosta turnoff, you'll
see a "handpapersbruk" sign). If you've never seen handmade paper produced, this is free and worth a stop. Pick
up the English brochure or ask for a tour. Wide open June
through August, kind of open in the off-season.
▲**The Kingdom of Crystal**—This is Sweden's glass
country. Frankly, these glassworks cause so much excite-
ment because of the relative rarity of anything else thrilling in Sweden outside of greater Stockholm. (Remember,
I'm Norwegian.) Pick up the brochures in Vaxjo. I'd see a
small traditional *glasbruk* (glassworks) and then visit the
shop and museum of Orrefors.

The Bergdala glasbruk (30 minutes east of Vaxjo, leave
road 25 at Hovmantorp, drive 3 miles north, 9:00-14:30,
no action from 12:00-12:30, tel. 0478/11650) offers a fine
close-up look at actual craftsmen blowing and working
the red-hot glass, a good shop (with Bergdala's tempting
blue-ringed cereal bowls), and a fine picnic area with
covered tables if it's wet.

Of the several renowned glassworks, Orrefors is the
most famous but is quite a tourist racket and offers lousy
tours. They give three English tours a day (call 0481/34000
for times). Most visitors just observe the work from plat-
forms. The shop sells nearly perfect crystal seconds at a
fraction of the normal price—but it still ain't cheap.
(Open July Monday-Friday 9:00-19:00, Saturday
9:00-16:00, Sunday 11:00-16:00, off-season closing an
hour earlier.) Don't miss the dazzling "museum" (open
same hours as shop).

For a small traditional glasbruk near Orrefors, visit Gul-
laskruv Glasbruk in Halleberga. There are lots of other
glassworks. Most are open for viewing on workdays from
10:00 to 15:00.

Kalmar
Kalmar feels formerly strategic and important. Its salty
old center has a wistful sailor's charm. This, with its busy
waterfront, fine castle, and museum, makes it an excellent

last piece of small town Sweden before we plunge into Stockholm. In its day, Kalmar was called the gateway to Sweden. Today, it's just a sleepy has-been, "gateway" only to the holiday island of Oland.

The Kalmar Tourist Office (Larmgatan 6, tel. 0480/15350, open Monday-Friday 9:00-19:00 mid-June through mid-August, Saturday 9:00-17:00, Sunday 12:00-17:00, closing at 17:00 other months and closed on winter weekends) is very central and helpful. Get the handy town map and confirm your sightseeing plans. Kalmar's summer is from about mid-June through mid-August.

Sightseeing Highlights

▲▲▲ **Kalmar Castle**—This moated castle is one of Europe's great medieval experiences. The stark exterior, cuddled by a lush park, houses a fine Renaissance palace interior, which is the work of King Gustavus Vasa. The elaborately furnished rooms are entertainingly explained in English, and a more extensive guidebook is available for 15 kr. Notice how the electric candles "flicker." Open daily 10:00-18:00, Sunday 13:00-17:00 from mid-June to mid-August. Off-season— 10:00-16:00, Sunday 13:00-16:00, 20 kr, tel. 0480/56351.

▲▲ **Kalmar Provincial (Lans) Museum**—This museum houses the impressive salvaged wreck of the royal ship *Kronan*, which sank nearby in 1676. Lots of interesting soggy bits and old pieces with a "here's the buried treasure" thrill but unfortunately no information in English (borrow the *Kronan* exhibit in English text). See the excellent 12-minute English film (hourly, get times as you enter). Upstairs you'll also find a good Swedish design exhibit. Right downtown on the waterfront, open Monday through Saturday 10:00 to 18:00, Sunday 13:00 to 17:00, shorter hours and closed Mondays off-season. 20 kr, tel. 0480/56300.

▲▲ **The Island of Oland**—Europe's longest bridge (4 miles, free) connects Oland with Kalmar and the mainland. The island (90 miles long and only 8 miles wide) is a pleasant local resort known for its birds, windmills,

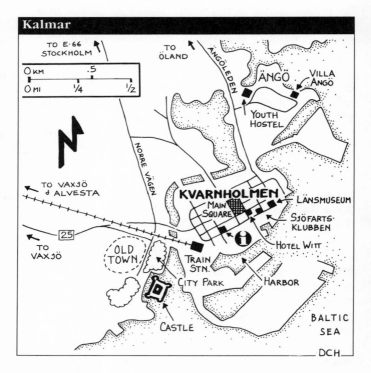

flowers, beaches, and prehistoric sights. Public transportation is miserable here, and the island is only worthwhile
if you have a car and 3 extra hours. A 60-mile circle south
of the bridge will give you a good dose of the island's
windy rural charm. The **Gettlinge Gravfalt** (just off the
road about ten miles up from the south tip) is a wonderfully situated boat-shaped Iron Age grave site littered
with monoliths, overseen by a couple of creaky old
windmills. It offers a commanding view of the windy and
mostly treeless island.

Farther south is the **Eketorp Prehistoric Fort**.
Eketorp is a very reconstructed fifth-century stone fort
that, as Iron Age forts go, is fairly interesting. Several
evocative huts and buildings are filled with what someone imagines may have been the style back then, and the
huge rock fort is surrounded by runty piglike creatures

that were common here 1,500 years ago. ("For your con-
venience and pleasure," the sign reads, "don't leave your
children alone with the animals.") Open daily 9:00-17:00,
English tours normally at 13:00. 20 kr, tel. 0485/34560.

Accommodations
Private rooms: The tourist office can always find you a
room in a private home (150 kr per double, no breakfast,
30 kr service fee). They can also get you special last-
minute discounts on fancy hotels.

Youth Hostel (IYHF): A fifteen-minute walk from the
center, this is a wonderful hostel run by Torsten Knutsson
and family. Two- or four-bed rooms, TV and sauna, lots
of extra facilities (73 kr per person, 30 kr breakfast).
Closed from 10:00 to 16:30. Torsten also runs a "hotel"
annex, the **Kalmar Lagprishotell Svanen**, with 330 kr
doubles including sheets and breakfast. (STF Vandrarhem,
Rappegatan 1, 39230 Kalmar, tel. 0480/12928.) You'll see
a blue and white hotel sign and hostel symbol at the edge
of town on Angoleden Street, less than a mile from the
station.

Sjofartsklubben (Seaman's Club)—In June, July, and
August, old Mr. Persson opens his clean, salty dormlike
place up to tourists. (It's the home of student sailors during the school year.) He has one- to five-bed rooms with
kitchen privileges and a lively common room. He doesn't
speak English, but this place is worth the struggle. Only
150 kr per double plus 30 kr for sheets. Olaudsgaten 45,
tel. 0480/10810, facing the harbor.

Hotel Villa Ango—This big old house on the water
ten minutes out of town has great facilities and 400 kr
doubles. Bagensgatan 20, tel. 0480/85415.

Soderportsgarden (250 kr doubles, breakfast extra,
Slottsvagen 1, tel. 0480/12501) is a university dorm that
opens up from June 10 to August 20 for tourists. It's beautifully located a block from the castle.

Hotel Witt (Sodra Langgatan 42, tel. 0480/15250) is a
classy place with an affordable summer price of 660 kr
per double with breakfast. If you arrive late, the TI can
often get you a "last minute special" here for about 520 kr.

Food

Eating on a budget in Kalmar is tough. The Domus
Department Store's **4 Kok** cafeteria serves cheap meals
right downtown. Open until 19:00 in summer. Pizza, Chinese food, salad bars, or the cafe in the Stroget mall just
off Storgatan are your best budget bets otherwise.

Byttan Restaurant—For a splurge, head out to the
castle to enjoy a great waterfront terrace for a 120 kr meal
or memorable cup of coffee.

Itinerary Option

We've got two nights and a day to explore this part of
Sweden. The aggressive option is to spend the first night
in Vaxjo, see its sights, and tour the glassworks. Get to
Kalmar early in the afternoon and skip Oland. The easy
option gives you two nights settled in Kalmar and covers
Oland and Kalmar rather than Vaxjo, glassworks, and
Kalmar. I like the first plan unless the immigration center
and the glass show don't interest you.

Also, think ahead to your Helsinki cruise. Boat tickets
may be cheaper (off-weekend) and your drive to Oslo
more reasonable (earlier start) if you do the Helsinki
excursion immediately after Kalmar and before seeing
Stockholm.

DAY 6

KALMAR TO STOCKHOLM

Today is basically a long drive. We'll leave early, stop for a leisurely lunch, and walk along the famous Gota Canal, then drive into Stockholm in time to visit the tourist office, get comfortably set up, tour the charming old town, and enjoy an atmospheric dinner.

Suggested Schedule	
8:00	Begin five-hour drive north along the coast to Stockholm.
10:30	Break in Vestervik.
12:00	Stop in Soderkoping for a picnic lunch and a walk along the Gota Canal.
13:30	Continue the trek north.
16:00	Arrive in Stockholm, visit tourist office to confirm plans, and set up.
18:30	Catch the Gamla Stan (Old Town) walking tour.
20:30	Dinner at Kristina Restaurant in Old Town.

Transportation

Highway E-66 takes you from Kalmar to Stockholm— follow E-66 Norrkoping signs. It's 240 miles and takes about 5 hours. Sweden did a cheap widening job, paving the shoulders of the old two-lane road to get about 3.8 lanes. Still, the traffic is polite and sparse and there's little to see or do, so stock the pantry (your "auto-mat"), set the compass on north, and home in on Stockholm.

Consider two pleasant stops along the way. Ninety miles north is Vastervik, with a pleasant eighteenth-century core of wooden houses (park at the little market on the waterfront where the center hits the lake). Soder-koping (150 miles north of Kalmar) is just right for a "lunch on the Gota Canal" stop. Stay on E-66 past the town center, turn right at the TI/Kanalbatarna/Slussen sign. Park by the canal. E-66 takes you to Norrkoping where you'll follow the E-4 signs winding through Norr-koping, then to Stockholm. The city "centrum" is clearly marked. (Following the signs into Stockholm is easier if you familiarize yourself with the areas on the inset of my "Greater Stockholm" map. Even then, without a map, plan on getting lost.)

▲ **Gota Canal and Soderkoping**—Sweden's famous Gota Canal is 110 miles of lakes and canals cutting Sweden in half with 58 locks (slussen) working slowly up to a summit of 300 feet. It was built 150 years ago with over 7 million 12-hour man-days (60,000 men working about 22 years) at a low ebb in the country's self-esteem . . . to show her industrial oats. Today it's a lazy 3- or 4-day tour for experts in lethargy. We'll just take a quick peak at the Gota Canal over lunch as it passes through the medieval town of Soderkoping.

The TI on Radhustorget (a square about a block off the canal) has good English town maps and canal information. From there go to the canal. The Toalett sign points to the "Kanulbatiquen," a yachters' laundry, shower, shop, and WC with idyllic canalside picnic tables. Munch down. Just to the right is a lock. From there a series of stairs leads up to the Utsiktsplats pavilion (a nice view, not quite worth the hike unless you need the exercise). From the canal, a lane leads into town to the pleasant Hagatorget (square) and return to your car.

Stockholm

If I had to call one European city "home," it would be Stockholm. Green, clean, efficient, and surrounded by as much water as land, Sweden's capital is underrated, landing just above Bordeaux, Brussels, and Bucharest on many tourist checklists. I rank it with Amsterdam, Munich, and Madrid.

While progressive and sleek, Stockholm respects its heritage. Throughout the summer mounted bands parade each noontime through the heart of town to the royal palace announcing the changing of the guard and turning even the most dignified tourist into a scampering kid. The Gamla Stan (Old Town) celebrates the Midsummer festivities (late June) with the down-home vigor of a rural village, forgetting that it's the core of a gleaming twentieth-century metropolis.

Greater Stockholm's 1.4 million residents live on fourteen islands, but visitors need only concern themselves with five: Norrmalm (downtown, with most hotels, shopping areas, and the train station), Gamla Stan (the old city of winding lantern-lit streets, antique shops, and classy glassy cafes clustered around the royal palace), Sodermalm (aptly called Stockholm's "Brooklyn," residential and untouristy), Skeppsholmen (the small, very central traffic-free park island with the Modern Art Museum and two fine youth hostels), and Djurgarden (literally "deer garden," Stockholm's wonderful green playground, with many of the city's top sights).

Tourist Information
Hotel Centralen—Basically a room-finding service (located downstairs in the central station), Hotel Centralen's friendly staff also handles your sightseeing and transportation questions. This is the place to arrange your accommodations, buy your Tourist Card, and pick up free brochures: city map, "This Week in Stockholm" (which lists opening hours and directions to all the sights and special events), and whatever else you need (free English brochures on city walks, camping, parking, jazz boats, excursions, bus routes, shopping, etc.). Confirm your sightseeing plans. Long hours—May-September 8:00-21:00 daily; off-season—Monday-Friday 8:30-16:45 only; tel. 08/240880.

Sweden House (Sverige Huset)—Europe's most creative and energetic tourist information office is a short walk from the station on Kungstradgarden. A patient local expert will answer all your questions. They've got pamphlets on everything; an "excursion shop" for transportation, day trip and bus tour information, and tickets; a national section for information on Sweden outside of Stockholm; and an English library and reading room upstairs with racks of 1 kr information on various aspects of Swedish Culture. Tel. 221840 gets you their recorded

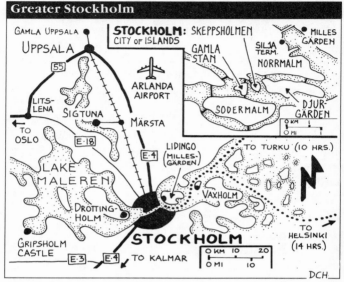

Greater Stockholm

"What's on Today" message. Open June-August, Monday-
Friday 8:30-18:00, Saturday-Sunday 8:00-17:00; off-
season, Monday-Friday 9:00-17:00, Saturday-Sunday
9:00-14:00. (Hamngatan 27, tel. 08/7892000, T-bana:
Kuugstradgarden.)

Transportation and the Stockholm Card

Stockholm is the complete hostess. She complements her
many sightseeing charms with great information services,
a fine bus and subway system, and special passes to take
the bite out of the city's cost (or at least limit it to one
vicious budgetary gash).

   Go-as-you-please passes called "Tourist Cards" are
available at TIs and newsstands. They give you free run of
all public transport for 24 hours (28 kr) or 72 hours (95 kr,
this one includes the harbor ferry and admission to Skansen, Grona Lund, and the Post Tower, called Kaknastor-
net). If you decide to buy individual tickets, consider the
cheaper ten-ride strip cards, and remember, each ticket
(10 kr) is valid for one hour. The subway, called T-bana or
tunnelbana, gets you where you want to go very quickly.

   Stockholm's "Tourist Line" bus route, departing every

10 minutes, does a figure eight hitting 14 major sights. This lets you get off and on as you please, to "do the circuit" at your leisure. The "Tourist Line" brochure explains exactly how this 30 kr, 24-hour pass works.

Be sure to take advantage of the fun and handy boat connections from Nybroplan and Slussen to Djurgarden landing next to the Vasa and Skansen.

Busy sightseeing families save time and money with the Stockholm Card. This 24-hour (125 kr), 48-hour (190 kr), or 72-hour (285 kr) pass gives you and two children free run of all the public transit, free entry to virtually every sight, cheap parking, a good map, and a handy sightseeing handbook (sold at the TI). It could save even a single traveler money if you plan to do a 48-hour marathon of museum going and bus riding (admissions to the busiest two days of sightseeing alone would add up to about 200 kr).

Parking: Only a Swedish meatball would drive his car in Stockholm. Park it and use the public transit. But parking here is a major hassle and expense. Unguarded lots generally aren't safe. Take everything into your hotel or hostel or pay for a garage. The tourist office has a "Parking in Stockholm" brochure. Those hosteling on Skeppsholmen feel quite privileged with their 10-kr-a-day island parking passes. Those with the Stockholm Card can park in a very big central garage for the duration of the ticket for only 10 kr a day (rather than the normal 70-kr rate). Get your parking ticket and specifics at the Sweden House. There is a big, safe, and reasonable (10 kr per day) garage at Ropsten—the last subway station (near the Silja line terminal) and in the right end of town for your departure to Uppsala. If you'll be sailing to Finland, you can solve all your parking worries in a snap by long-term parking your car on arrival in Stockholm at either terminal's safe and reasonable parking lot. Park carefully. On my last trip, I got a 500 kr parking fine.

Bikes and Laundry: The Sommar Cafe (by the hostels on Skeppsholmen island, near the Sweden House) is a good example of what a people-oriented government can do with a high tax rate. This handy cafe is also a tourist information office and rents bikes (50 kr a day,

cheapest in town) and will do your laundry (20 kr a small
load, you put it in, they do the rest, call or drop in to
make an appointment with the machine). It's open Monday through Friday 10:00 to 18:00, Saturday 10:00 to
16:00, tel. 214548.

Accommodations

Stockholm has plenty of money-saving deals for the
savvy visitor. Its youth hostels are among Europe's best
($15 a bed). It has plenty of people offering private accom-
modations ($40 doubles). And peak season for Stock-
holm's expensive hotels is business time—workdays outside of summer. You'll find great deals on classy hotels
($100 doubles) by visiting during summer (mid-June
through mid-August) or on Friday, Saturday, or Sunday
nights. And to sort through all of this, the city has helpful,
English-speaking room-finding services with handy locations and long hours.

Hotel Centralen in the central station, lower level, for a
20 kr fee can nearly always find suitable rooms for those
who arrive without reservations. They also have special
discount possibilities and packages that can land you in
an impossibly expensive hotel almost affordably. And
they know exactly what's available in the realm of budget
and "sleep-in" alternatives to hotels (see above for hours
and phone). The Stockholm Tourist Office at the Sweden
House (see above, tel. 08/7892000, open daily) also books
rooms—but not quite as well. For room-finding, use Sweden
House only on weekends, when Centralen is closed.

Stockholm's tourist offices refer people in search of a
room in a private house to one of two agencies, Hotel-
janst (Vasagatan 15, tel. 08/104467) and Allrum (Wallinga-
tan 34, tel. 08/213789). Each can set you up for about 250
kr per double, minimum two nights, no fee. If you'd like
to go direct, Mrs. Lindstrom (T-bana: Islandstorget, tel.
371608) runs a pleasant B&B.

Hotels

Queen's Hotel is cheery, clean, and just a ten-minute
walk from the station, in a great pedestrian area across the

street from the Centralbadet (city baths). This is probably the best cheap hotel in town (doubles with breakfast 460-560 kr in summer, 590-690 kr in winter, Drottninggatan 71A, tel. 08/24 94 60).

Hotel Berma, also near the station, is modern, clean and friendly. Ask for their "comfort" room and a weekend rate even on a weekday and eat pizza next door to save some money (doubles with breakfast 500-600 kr, Upplandsgatan 13, S-11123 Stockholm, tel. 08/23 26 75).

Hotel Karelia—This stately old Finnish-run hotel is centrally located, not as bright and quiet as Queen's but a good value for a "normal" hotel. Swimming pool and sauna (open to public, cheaper for guests). Doubles are around 600 kr in summer, 900 in winter. 35 Birger Jarlsgatan, tel. 247660. The windowless "cabin" rooms are cheapest.

Jerum Hotel—This huge, sleek, and clean university dorm offers 120 double rooms during the summer break (June, July, and August only) for about 300 kr. It's not central, but just ride the subway to Gardet and walk through the park. Studentbacken 21, tel. 635380.

Hotel Frescati—Another huge June-to-August-only hotel offering singles and doubles with showers for around 130 kr per person. Professorslingen 13, T-bana: Universitetet, tel. 158742.

Two cheap, dreary, but sleepable little hotels at the Odenplan subway stop offering doubles with breakfast in the summer for around 400 kr are **Pensionat Oden** (Odengatan 38, tel. 306349) and **Hotel Gustav Wasa** (Vastmannagatan 61, tel. 343801).

Hotel Anno 1647 is a typical old Swedish hotel with a few cheaper rooms without showers. This is just off the Old Town near Slussen (under the Katarina elevator) and is a good splurge (600 kr doubles in summer, Mariagrand 3, tel. 08/44 04 80).

Youth Hostels
Stockholm has a tremendous selection of hostels offering good beds in simple but interesting places for from 70 to 120 kr. If your budget is tight, these are great. Each has a

helpful English-speaking staff, pleasant family rooms, good facilities, and helpful leads on budget survival in Stockholm and will hold rooms for a phone call. Nonmembers are welcome, but with sheet rental (25 kr once) and the nonmember's fee (28 kr a night) and breakfast (40 kr), they save only about $15 per person over the hotels.

Af Chapman (IYHF)—1988 was the centennial year of Europe's most famous youth hostel, the permanently moored cutter ship *Af Chapman*. Just a five-minute walk from downtown, this floating hostel has 140 beds—two to eight per stateroom. It's a compassionate place and saves at least 30 beds each morning for unreserved arrivals. So if you call at breakfast time and show up before 9:00 you should land a bed even in summer. The place is run simple but friendly. A great young but warm atmosphere prevails. Study the warden's personal scrapbook of budget Stockholm information. Ask about discounts on boat tours. Open April to mid-December, 7:00 to 12:00 and 15:00 to 01:00, with a lounge and a cafeteria that welcomes even nonhostelers from 8:00 to 10:00 (summer only) and 12:00 to 18:00. STF Vandranhem "Af Chapman," Skeppsholmen, 11149 Stockholm, tel. 103715.

Skeppsholmen Hostel (IYHF)—Just ashore from the *Af Chapman*, this hostel is open all year. It has better facilities and smaller rooms (many doubles), but it isn't as romantic as its seagoing sister. Tel. 202506. While they take no phone reservations, you should call to see what's available.

Zinken Hostel (IYHF)—This is a big, basic, well-run hostel with nearly all doubles, a sauna, a laudromat, and the best hostel kitchen facilities in town. In a busy suburb (T-bana: Hornstull or Zinkensdamm). STF Vandrarhem Zinken, Zinkens Vag 20, tel. 6685786. Open 7:00 to 23:00, all year. A great no-nonsense value.

Langholmen Youth Hostel (IYHF) and Hotel—If you ever wanted to sleep in a real prison and keep the key, this is for you. This "Swedish Alcatraz" has been converted into a 272-bed (in doubles and quads) hostel. It's actually quite classy but inconvenient for public transportation (undoubtedly a hangover from its prison days).

(Kronohaktet, Langholmen Island, T-Bana to Hornstull and a 10-minute walk, tel. 688-0510).

Vandrarhemmet Brygghuset—A former brewery near Odenplan, open from June 15 to August 15 daily 8:00 to 12:00 and 15:00 to 22:00 (no curfew). Its 2- to 6-bed rooms are open to all. Norrtullsgatan 12 N., tel. 312424.

Columbus Hotel and Hostel—This plain, well-run, no-smoking-allowed hostel is a historic old building in a park next to a police station. Mostly 4- and 6-bed rooms with a few doubles. Near T-bana: Medborgarplatsen, Tjarhovsgatan 11, tel. 441717.

International Youth Center (40 kr per bed, Valhallavagen 142, near Karlaplan, tel. 663-4389, open mid-June through August) rents about the cheapest dorm beds in town.

Camping
Stockholm has seven campgrounds (located south of town) that solve your parking and budget problems wonderfully. The TI's "Camping Stockholm" brochure has specifics.

Food
Breakfast: Don't miss downtown Stockholm's budget miracle—the famous "Frukostbuffet" (smorgasbord breakfast) in the central station. Under the huge "Restaurang" sign in the main hall, the **Centralens Restaurang** offers an elegant 50 kr all-you-can-eat feast every morning in Orient Express atmosphere. (Monday-Saturday 6:30-10:00, closed all of July, tel. 20 20 49).

Lunch: Stockholm's elegant department stores (notably Ahlens near Sergelstorg) have cafeterias for the crown-pinching local shopper. Look for the around 50 kr daily specials called "Dagens ratt" (no, it doesn't mean "rodent of the day"). Monday through Friday from 11:00 to 17:00, the City Hall **Kalleren Restaurant (Stadshuskallaren)** serves up a decent 50 kr lunch (prepared by the same folks who prepare the Nobel Prize banquet). The cafe on the *Af Chapman* youth hostel (open to the public daily from 12:00-18:00) serves a good salad/roll/coffee lunch in unbeatable atmosphere if the weather's good.

Dinner: "Husmans Kost" means typical Swedish cuisine. Cafes serve the cheapest light meals. **Lyktan** (just
behind the Grand Hotel at Teatergatan 6, near the Skeppsholmen hostels) serves a salad bar, cracker spread, and
main course from 11:00 to 21:00 Monday through Friday,
for 50 kr. The atmosphere is musty, the TV is on, the people are friendly, and the price is unbeatable.

In the Old Town (Gamla Stan), don't miss the wonderfully atmospheric **Kristina Restaurang** (Vesterlanggatan
68, Gamla Stan, tel. 200529). In this 1632 building under
a leather ceiling and steeped in a turn-of-the-century
interior, you'll find good dinners from 60 kr. From 11:00
to 15:00 they serve a great 50 kr lunch—entrée, salad bar,
bread, and drink. The place is best Wednesday through
Saturday from 20:00 to 23:00 when live jazz accompanies
your meal. You can enjoy the music cheaply over just a
beer or coffee, too.

Survival by Picnic: With higher and higher taxes
almost every year, Sweden's restaurant industry is really
suffering. You'll notice many fine places almost empty.
Swedes joke that the local cuisine is now Chinese, Italian,
and hamburgers. Here more than anywhere, budget
travelers should picnic. A quick sandwich and hard-
boiled egg tucked into your zip-lock at breakfast for
lunch, a box of drink, yogurt, and fruit from the market,
whatever, prepared food is going to be quite expensive
and picnicking lets you fill up cheaply.

The market at **Hotortorget** is a fun place to picnic
shop, especially in the indoor and exotic ethnic Hotorgs-
hallen. The outdoor market closes up at 18:00, and many
merchants put their unsold produce on the push list.
Stockholm's major department stores and the many small
corner groceries are all fine places to assemble a good
picnic spread. The supermarket downstairs in the central
train station is open late (Monday-Friday 7:00-23:00,
Saturday and Sunday 9:00-23:00) and is filled with great
picnic stuff, even fresh ready-made sandwiches.

STOCKHOLM

Stockholm tempts many to toss out the itinerary and settle in forever. Green, built on fourteen islands, surrounded by water and woods, bubbling with energy and history, it fills two days to the brim with memorable sights and experiences. On Day 7, we'll crawl through Europe's best-preserved old warship, tour Europe's first and best open-air folk museum, and get a pleasant overview of the city by taking a canal boat tour.

Day 8 focuses on today's Stockholm with its marvelous city hall, modern department stores, art museums, and futuristic planned suburbs. You'll have some hard choices to make to catch the 18:00 boat to Finland. Europe's most enjoyable cruise begins with lovely archipelago scenery, a setting sun, and a royal smorgasbord dinner.

Suggested Schedule Day 7	
9:00	Confirm your plans at the Sweden House. Buy a picnic lunch in the basement of the NK department store across the street. Walk through the Kungstradgarden to the docks.
10:00	"Under the Bridges" boat tour (from Grand Hotel).
11:00	Catch bus #47 to tour the big, palacelike Nordic Museum.
12:30	Skansen for a picnic lunch, catch the open-air folk museum tour (in English, usually on the hour).
16:00	*Vasa*: see the English-subtitled movie and catch the English tour right afterward (each go on the half-hour for 25 minutes).
Evening	Back at Skansen for folk music and dancing or a cruise with dinner and jazz. Ask for timely advice at TI.

Suggested Schedule Day 8	
8:00	Breakfast, and fill your zip-lock at breakfast for a light lunch (save room for your buffet dinner).
10:00	Enjoy the city hall's entertaining guided tour.
11:00	Climb the city hall tower for Stockholm's best view. Walk to the palace via the bridge at the end of Drottningsgatan (or if you're early follow the parade over Strombron, two bridges farther down).
12:00	Catch the changing of the guard at the palace. Then tour the royal palace apartments and crown jewels. Picnic on Stromparterren under the Norrbro bridge (consider the city medieval museum while you're there).
15:00	Browse through the modern city center, around Kungstradgarden, Sergels Torg and Drottningsgatan area. Visit Kulturhuset, NK or Ahlens department store, walk up to the Hotorget market and indoor food hall, or go shopping in the Gamla Stan.
17:00	Board your boat, shower, rest.
18:30	Enjoy the island wonderland, smorgasbord dinner, and a Scandinavian sunset.

Sightseeing Highlights—Downtown Stockholm

▲Kungstradgarden—The "King's Garden" square is the downtown people-watching center. Watch the life-sized game of chess, enjoy the free concerts at the bandstand. Surrounded by the Sweden House, the NK department store, the harborfront and tour boats, grab the first blond you see and feel Stockholm's pulse.

▲Sergels Torg—The heart of modern Stockholm, just between Kungstradgarden and the station, is worth a wander. Enjoy the colorful and bustling underground mall and the "Kulturhuset," a center for reading, relaxing, and socializing designed for normal people but welcoming tourists. You'll enjoy music, exhibits, hands-on fun, and an insight into contemporary Sweden. (Free, daily from 11:00 to 17:00, often later)

▲▲**City Hall**—The "Stadshuset" is a very impressive mix of 8 million bricks, 19 million chips of gilt mosaic, and lots of Stockholm pride. One of Europe's most impressive modern (1923) buildings and site of the annual Nobel Prize dinner, it's particularly enjoyable and worthwhile for its entertaining tours (daily at 10:00 and 12:00, often at 11:00 and 14:00, call 785-9000, just behind the station). Be sure to climb the 350-foot tower for the best city view possible (10:00-15:00, May-September). The City Hall also has a helpful TI.

▲**Orientation Views**—Try to get a bird's-eye perspective on this wonderful urban mix of water, parks, concrete, and people from the City Hall tower (see above), the Kaknas Tower (at 500 feet, it's the tallest building in Scandinavia, daily May-August 9:00-24:00, until 22:00 in April and September, 15 kr, tel. 789 24 35, bus #69 from Nybroplan), or the top of the Katarina Elevator (near Slussen subway stop, 3 kr, then walk behind along Katarinavagen through classy homes and grand views). For a quick big-bus orientation tour, consider those that leave from the Royal Opera House (50 minutes, 50 kr, 4 times a day).

▲▲**Under the Bridges Canal Tour**—For the best 90-minute, 70 kr floating look at Stockholm—and a pleasant break—consider this cruise. Tour boats leave on the hour from 10:00 to 19:00 from in front of the Grand Hotel. On many boats the open seats in the rear offer the most vibration and exhaust until the boat leaves. Then they become the best seats on board. The *Af Chapman* hostel usually has discount tickets for city harbor tours (40% off).

▲**National Museum**—It's mediocre by European standards but small, central, uncrowded, and very user-friendly. The highlights are several Rembrandts, a fine group of impressionists, and works by the popular and very good-to-get-to-know local artists Carl Larsson and

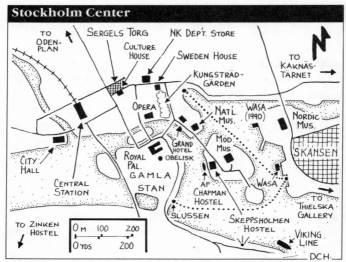

Stockholm Center

TO ODEN-PLAN • SERGELS TORG • NK DEP'T. STORE • CULTURE HOUSE • SWEDEN HOUSE • KUNGSTRÄD-GÄRDEN • TO KAKNÄS-TÄRNET → • OPERA • NATL. MUS. • WASA (1990) • NORDIC MUS. • CITY HALL • GRAND HOTEL • MOD. MUS. • SKANSEN • ROYAL PAL. • OBELISK • CENTRAL STATION • GAMLA STAN • AF CHAPMAN HOSTEL • WASA • TO ZINKEN HOSTEL • SLUSSEN • SKEPPSHOLMEN HOSTEL • THIELSKA GALLERY • VIKING LINE • 0 M 100 200 • 0 YDS 200 • DCH

Anders Zorn. Tuesday 10:00-21:00, Wednesday-Sunday
10:00-17:00. Closed Monday. In July and August, open
Tuesday until 17:00 because of special concerts. 30 kr, tel.
666 42 50.

Museum of Modern Art—This bright and cheery
gallery is as far out as can be, with Picasso, Braque, and
lots of goofy dada art (such as the "urinal" and the "goat
with tire"). In a pleasant park on Skeppsholmen. Open
Tuesday-Friday 11:00-21:00, Saturday-Sunday 11:00-17:00,
closed Monday, 20 kr (free on Thursday).

Gamla Stan (Old Town) Sights
▲▲**Gamla Stan**—Stockholm's old island core is charming, fit for a film, and full of antique shops, street lanterns, painted ceilings, and surprises. Spend some time
here, browse, enjoy a cafe, get to know a shopkeeper. The
impressive Royal Palace is tourable—crown jewels and
lavish apartments. A military parade culminates at the palace for the changing of the guard, a daily 12:00 thrill
(13:00 on Sunday). The Riddarholm Church is the final
resting place for about 600 years of Sweden's royalty
(open 10:00-15:00, Sunday 13:00-15:00, May-August, less
in September, 5 kr, tel. 789-8500).

▲ **Royal Palace**—The stately exterior encloses 608 rooms of glittering baroque and rococo decor. If you like palaces, don't miss this one. There are eight different sights with separate admissions here. Most important are the apartments, open Tuesday through Saturday 10:00 to 15:00, Sunday 12:00 to 15:00, mid-May through mid-August, from noon the rest of the year, 15 kr. The Royal Treasury is another ticket (similar hours, no samples).

Riksdag—You can tour Sweden's parliament buildings if you'd like a firsthand look at its government. (Tours in English throughout the summer, usually Monday-Friday at 12:30 and 15:00, but call 786-4000 to confirm. Free.)

▲ **Old Town Walking Tour**—For an informal, chatty, and historic walk, join gracious and eccentric (she'll take that as a compliment) Klara, or one of her fellow guides, on a two-hour Gamla Stan tour. Tours depart daily (rain or shine) at 18:30 from the "Obelisk" next to the palace. Groups are very small. Just show up. (If you're late, she talks for a while at the obelisk before heading out.) She chatters on in a grandmotherly effervescent way. After a few doubtful moments, you'll feel good about the fluffy experience and leave with a better understanding of the very historic Gamla Stan.

Djurgarden Sightseeing Highlights

▲▲▲ **Skansen**—Europe's original and best open-air folk museum, Skansen is a huge park gathering over 150 historic buildings (homes, churches, schoolhouses, etc.) transplanted from all corners of Sweden. Tourists can explore this Swedish culture on a lazy Susan, seeing folk crafts in action and wonderfully furnished old interiors. In the town quarter (top of the escalator), potters, glassblowers, and other craftspeople are busy doing their traditional thing. Free and excellent one-hour guided walks paint a fine picture of old Swedish life-styles (usually at 12:00, 14:00, and 16:00 daily mid-June through August, from the Bollnastorget meeting place, call to confirm). There's folk dancing every summer weekday at 19:00 and Sundays at 14:30 and 16:00.

Kids love Skansen, especially its zoo (ride a Dalarna

horse and stare down a hedgehog) and Lill' Skansen
(Punch 'n Judy, mini-train, and pony ride fun daily from
10:00 to 16:00). There are lots of special events, several
restaurants (the Solliden Vardhuset self-service offers uniformly good food, value, and a view), picnic benches
(especially at Torshinden), and great people-watching.
Pick up the 5 kr map as you enter and drop by the Bollnastorget information desk to confirm your Skansen
plans. Depart by the west entrance (Hazeliusporten) if
you're heading for the Nordic Museum. Open May
through August 9:00 to 22:00 (buildings 1l:00-17:00);
winter 9:00 to 17:00 (buildings 11:00-15:00). 22 kr entry
(16 kr in winter). Telephone 663 0500 for today's tour,
music, and dance schedule. You can miss Grona Lund,
the second-rate amusement park across the street.

▲▲▲**Vasa**—Stockholm turned a titanic flop into one of
Scandinavia's great sightseeing attractions—and
experiences. This glamorous but unseaworthy warship
sank a few minutes into its maiden voyage in 1628. After
333 years, it rose again from the deep (with the help of
marine archaeologists), and today it's the best-preserved
ship of its kind anywhere. Catch the 25-minute English
tours (on the half hour in summer) and the 25-minute
movie (on the other half hour) to best enjoy and understand the ship. Learn about "ship's rules" (bread can't be
older than 8 years), why it sank (heavy bread?), how it's
preserved, and so on. Open daily from 9:30 to 19:00, off-
season 10:00 to 17:00, 15 kr. Take bus #47 just past the big
brick Nordic Museum, catch the boat, or walk from Skansen. Tel. 666-4870.

▲▲ **Nordic Museum**—Try hard to see this great look at
Scandinavian culture. Highlights include the "Food and
Drink" section with its stunning china and crystal table
settings, the Nordic folk art (2nd floor), and the huge
statue of Gustav Wasa, father of modern Sweden, by Carl
Milles (top of 2nd flight of stairs) and the Sami (Lapp)
exhibit, with their more clever than ever animal traps, in
the basement. Open 10:00 to 16:00, Tuesdays until 20:00,
Saturday and Sunday until 17:00, closed Fridays in winter.

20 kr admission. The 20 kr guidebook isn't necessary, but pick up the free maps at the entrance.

▲**Thielska Galleriet**—If you liked the Larsson and Zorn art in the National Gallery and/or if you're a Munch fan, this charming mansion on the water at the far end of the Djurgarten park is worth the trip. Bus #69 from Karlaplan or boat from center. Monday through Friday 12:00 to 16:00, Saturday and Sunday 13:00 to 16:00, 20 kr.

Sights Farther from the Center

▲▲**Carl Milles Garten**—This is the home and major work of Sweden's greatest sculptor, situated on a cliff overlooking the city. Milles's entertaining, unique, and provocative art was influenced by Rodin. Classy cafe, great picnic spot. T-bana to Ropsten, then bus #221 to Torsvik, getting off at Foresta. Open daily 10:00 to 17:00, shorter hours off-season, 25 kr. Tel. 731-5060.

▲**Drottningholm**—The queen's seventeenth-century summer castle and present royal residence has been called, not surprisingly, Sweden's Versailles. It's great, but if you saw Denmark's Frederiksborg Palace and you are rushed in Stockholm, skip this. The adjacent uncannily well preserved baroque theater is the real highlight here, especially with its guided tours (22 kr, English theater tours twice an hour May-September, about the same hours as the palace). Get there by a pleasant but over-priced boat ride (55 kr round-trip, two-hour) or take the subway to Brommaplan and the bus to Drottningholm. Palace and Theater open daily from 11:00 to 16:30, May through August; in September, daily from 12:30 to 15:00. Call 759-0310 for palace tours in English schedule, 20 kr.

The seventeenth-century Drottningholm court theater performs perfectly authentic operas (30 performances each summer). Tickets to these very popular and unique shows go on sale each March. Prices for this time-tunnel musical and theatrical experience are 75 to 400 kr. Ten or fifteen seats are sometimes held for sales at the door before the performance. For information, write in February to Drottningholm's Theater Museum, Box 27050, 10251 Stockholm, or phone 08/660-8281.

▲**Futuristic planned suburbs**—Stockholm, the birthplace of cradle-to-grave security, is also a trendsetter in jukebox-orderly orbit towns. Farsta, a model of 1960s urban town planning, is most famous, but Kista and Skarholmen (with a huge daily flea market and an Ikea department store filled with modern Swedish furniture) offer a more interesting peek into our too well organized urban future. (Just ride the subway to the suburb of your choice.)

▲▲**Archipelago**—24,000 of the world's most scenic islands surround Stockholm. Europeans who spend entire vacations in and around Stockholm rave about them. If you cruise to Finland, you'll get a good three-hour dose of this island beauty. Otherwise, consider the pleasant hour-long cruise (25 kr each way) from the Grand Hotel downtown to the quiet town of Vaxholm.

▲**Sauna**—Sometime while you're in Sweden or Finland you'll have to treat yourself to Scandinavia's answer to support hose and a face lift. (A sauna is actually more Finnish than Swedish.) "Simmer down" with the local students, retired folks, and busy executives. Try to cook as calmly as the Swedes. Just before bursting, go into the shower room. There's no "luke cold," and the "trickle down theory" doesn't apply—only one button bringing a Niagara of liquid ice. Suddenly your shower stall becomes a Cape Canaveral launch pad as your body scatters to every corner of the universe. A moment later you're back together. Rejoin the Swedes in the cooker, this time with their relaxed confidence; you now know that exhilaration is just around the corner. Only very rarely will you feel so good.

Any tourist office can point you toward the nearest birch twigs. Good opportunities on our tour include your Stockholm-Helsinki cruise, any major hotel you stay in (Hotel Karelia's is open to the public, 60 kr), some hostels, or, least expensively, a public swimming pool. In Stockholm, consider the Eriksdalsbadet at Hammarby Slussvag 8, near Skanstule T-bana. Use of its 50-meter pool and first-rate sauna costs 20 kr (for hours, tel. 433372).

For the royal treatment at a reasonable price, right downtown, visit the newly refurbished (from 1904) Centralbadet (open Monday-Friday 7:00-17:00, Saturday 10:00-16:00, Drottningsgatan 88, 5 minutes up from Sergels Torg, tel. 24 24 02). For 40 kr you'll get the sauna, pool, sym, solarium, "bubblepool," and a few other pieces of wet hedonism. Birch twigs and a massage will cost you a few more krowns.

Shopping

Caution: Shopping is a rich man's sport in Stockholm. Modern design, glass, clogs, and wood goods are popular targets for shoppers. Browsing is a delightful, free way to enjoy Sweden's brisk pulse. Cop a feel at the Nordiska Kompanient (NK) just across from the Sweden House or in the nearby Gallerian mall. Swedish stores are open from 8:00 to 18:00, only until 14:00 on Saturday, closed Sunday.

For fleas, visit the Loppmarknaden (flea market) at the planned suburb of Skarholmen (5 kr, Monday-Friday 11:00-18:00, Saturday 9:00-15:00, Sunday 10:00-15:00, busiest on weekends).

Sailing from Stockholm to Helsinki

Two fine and fiercely competitive lines, Viking and Silja, connect the capitals of Sweden and Finland daily and nightly. The scenic 14-hour passage passes through a fair number of the countless islands that buffer Stockholm from the open sea. Each line offers luxurious smorgasbord meals, reasonable cabins, plenty of entertainment (discos, saunas, gambling), and enough duty-free shopping to sink a ship.

The big and much discussed issue is, which line is best. You could count showers and compare shoeshines, but basically each line almost goes overboard to win the loyalty of the three and a half million duty-free-crazy Swedes and Finns who make the trip each year. I'd say it's too close to call.

For car travelers, the Viking Line offers very convenient Stockholm parking, more of the harbor to see on the cruise, a more centrally located terminal, bigger ships, and a little cheaper fare. Those with Eurailpasses should go Silja since the crossing is free with the pass (also, seniors, students with ISIC cards, and Interrail/boat pass travelers get 50% off; Nordtourist pass holders go to Turku free and pay 50% for the Helsinki trip). While Viking offers lesser discounts to train travelers, it plans to match Silja's deals in 1991.

Fares vary radically with the season. Peak season, from about June 20 through August 12, is most expensive ($50 each way; $180 for round-trip "cruise package" with two smorgasbord dinners, two huge breakfasts, and two nights in a four-bed cabin). Fares drop by 30 to 50 percent in off-season (about August 13 through June 19). Off-season Fridays are often classified as high season. If you're staying over a night in Helsinki, book your hotel through your boat line and save. There are fancier stateroom arrangements for more money. And remember to consider the "open-jaws" plan, sailing into Helsinki and home from Turku (with the cheaper round-trip boat fare and the discount train ticket you can get with the cruise ticket, it's no more expensive overall).

The fares are so cheap because they operate tax-free and because the hordes of locals who sail to shop and drink duty- and tax-free spend a fortune on board. Last year, the average passenger spent nearly as much on booze and duty-free items as he did for the boat fare. It's a very large operation—mostly for locals. The boats are filled with about 60 percent Finns, 35 percent Swedes, and 5 percent cruisers from other countries. The Pepsi and Coke of the Scandinavian cruise industry vie to outdo each other with bigger and fancier boats. The Viking's new *Cinderella* will be topped by two new Silja boats in 1991. The ships are big: 56,000 tons, nearly 200 yards long, and, with 2,500 beds, the largest (and some of the cheapest) luxury hotels in Scandinavia.

Cruise Tactics and Miscellany: Both lines sail daily in both directions leaving at 18:00, arriving the next morning at 9:00. They also sail from Turku (21:30) to

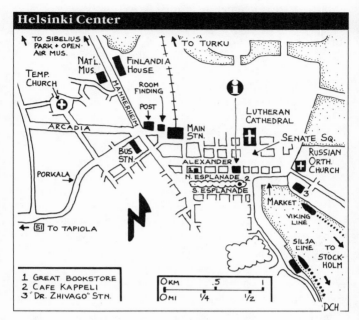

Stockholm (7:00) daily. There are morning departures, but, for our purposes, nighttime is the right time.

Reservations—Never necessary for deck class "walk-ons." Summer (June-August) and Fridays and Saturdays are most crowded for staterooms. I'd book the whole package at a travel agency in Copenhagen or Kalmar. It's easy and costs no more than going direct. You can call Viking (08/71 45 600) or Silja (08/22 21 40) in Stockholm.

Terminal Locations—In Stockholm, Viking is more central (free shuttle service on bus #45 from the Slussen T-bana stop), just past the Gamla Stan. You can normally see the huge red and white Viking ship parked in the harbor. For Silja, take the free and frequent bus from the central train station or from the Ropsten T-bahn station or ride the T-bana to "Gardet" and walk for about 10 minutes to the terminal. In Helsinki, both lines are perfectly central, ten minutes' walk from the market, Senate Square, and shopping district.

Parking—Both lines offer safe and handy 40 kr/day

parking. Viking's ticket machine takes 10 kr notes and 5 kr coins. Put your money in until you see the date and time of your return on the meter (it seems to work only in full-day increments). Then you hit the button and leave your ticket on your dashboard. Silja's lot is blessed with a human money taker. Consider parking your car here on arrival in Stockholm two days before you sail.

Terminal Buildings—These are well organized and functional, with facilities such as cafes, lockers, tourist information desks, lounges, and phones. Remember, two thousand passengers come and go with each boat. Customs is a snap—I have never shown my passport.

Meals—The cruise is famous for its smorgasbords—and understandably so. Board the ship hungry and prepare for a smorgasm. You'll pay about 110 kr for dinner and 50 kr for breakfast, each a great value for Scandinavia. These meals work out even cheaper with the mini-cruise package. Dinner is self-served in two sittings (I request the early one, with a window seat). The view is great from the table. Make a reservation on boarding. Remember, operate on Swedish time until you go to bed, then set your watch ahead an hour. Morning schedules are Finnish time (and vice versa when you return). Security is lax at breakfast, and if I don't stuff myself, I can rationalize packing a roll and cheese in my zip-lock baggie for lunch in very expensive Helsinki. There are also several classy à la carte restaurants on board.

Sleeping Free—Most boats have "sleep-ins" that are open dorms of as many as 200 free bunk beds. Call in advance to see if you can reserve one for your trip. Sometimes its "festival sleeping," in which case I'd board early and stake out my bed. Thirty minutes after departure unclaimed stateroom beds are rented for about $20 each. Each ship has a safe locked-from-port-to-port luggage area.

Day Privileges—If you're spending two nights in a row on the boat, you have access to your stateroom all day long. You can sleep in and linger over breakfast, if you like, long after the boat has docked. But, really, there's way too much to do in Helsinki to take advantage of these privileges (unless you take the round-trip passage twice, on four successive nights—a reasonable option given the high cost of hotels and meals on shore and the frustration of trying to see Helsinki in a day).

Sauna—Each ship has a sauna. This costs about 45 kr extra and you should reserve a time on boarding. Saunas are half price or even free in the morning.

Banking—The change desk on board is actually a better deal for small amounts of cash than using a Helsinki bank. (The boat rates are a hair lower, but banks charge 15 mk for cash and 20 for traveler's checks while the boat change desk does cash for no fee and 20 mk for checks. Just change some of your Swedish krowns for the day. There are about four Finnish marks in a U.S. dollar.)

Cruise Schedule	
17:00	Check in early. Pick up information about your ship and a Helsinki Guide. Reserve dinner, book Helsinki tour, change money into Finnmarks, move into your room, and explore the boat. Notice the nautical chart on the wall with your route marked. (Boarding starts 90 minutes before departure).
18:00	Be on deck or near a window to enjoy three hours of luxurious island scenery. The archipelago is one of Sweden's great sights.
18:00 or 20:30	Dinner. This is a sightseeing tour for your tongue. Take very small portions of everything in sight. More hot dishes often appear later. Don't miss the delicious dessert berries.
Late	Boogie, disco, waltz, or piano bar. Or study up on Helsinki.

HELSINKI

The boat is your hotel, and you've got all day to see the neoclassical capital of Finland. Start with the 2½-hour "Hello Helsinki" bus tour that meets the boat at the dock. Before disembarking, ask when your boat raises its gangplank tonight (Finnish time). You'll have the afternoon to enjoy Helsinki's ruddy harborfront market, count goosebumps in her churches, tour the national museum or the open-air folk museum. By dinnertime, you'll once again surround yourself with beautiful islands and lots of food.

Suggested Schedule	
9:30	On landing, catch the bus tour or take the city intro walk described below.
12:00	Mingle through the market, buy (and eat) a picnic, drop into the tourist office to confirm your plans.
13:00	Browse and people-watch through downtown to the National Museum.
15:00	Tour the National Museum or catch a bus to the open-air folk museum to catch the 15:30 English walking tour or take a harbor boat tour.
17:00	Enjoy a cup of coffee in the Cafe Kappeli before boarding time.
17:45	Sail away. Another good dinner smorgasbord.

Helsinki

Helsinki feels close to the Soviet Union. It is. Much of it reminds me of Leningrad. It's no wonder Hollywood chose to film *Dr. Zhivago*, *Reds*, and *Gorky Park* here. There is a huge and impressive Russian Orthodox church overlooking the harbor, a large Russian community, and several fine Russian restaurants. You'll see the "CCCP" (Soviet) train, which goes twice daily to Leningrad, in the station.

In the early 1800s when the Russians took Finland from Sweden, they moved the capital eastward from Turku, making Helsinki the capital of their "autonomous duchy." I asked a lady in the tourist office if a particular cafe was made for Russian officers. In a rare spasm of candor, she said, "All of nineteenth-century Helsinki was made for Russian officers."

Today Helsinki is gray and green. A little windy and cold, it looks like it's stuck somewhere in the north near the Russian border. But it makes the best of its difficult stuation and leaves the visitor impressed and glad he dropped in. It's a brisk walking and colorful shopping town of 500,000 people, one of Europe's first planned cities, which tends to turn guests into fans of town planning and architecture.

Finland's buildings, its design and fashions, and its people fit into their surroundings sensitively. Dissimilar elements are fused into a complex but comfortable whole. It's a very intimate and human place.

Finland's history as far as the sightseer is concerned is Swedish (before the 1809 Russian takeover, very little remains physically), Russian (1809-1917, when most of Helsinki's great buildings were built), and independent, when Finland's bold trendsetting modern design and architecture blossomed. Since World War II, Finland has teetered between independence and the U.S.S.R., treading very lightly on matters concerning her fragile autonomy and relations with her giant neighbor to the East. The recent collapse of the Warsaw Pact has made life in Helsinki more relaxed.

Weather: They say the people of Helsinki spend 9 months in winter and the other 3 months waiting for summer. The weather dictates a brief (June-August) tourist season. February in Finland is not my idea of a good time. It gets so cold that until recently, each winter, bus #19 extended its route over the frozen bay to a suburban island! When summer arrives, the entire population jumps in with street singing and beach blanket vigor.

Language: The only essential word for your quick visit is *Kiitos* (pron. "key toes")—that's "Thank you," and locals love to hear it.

Tourist Information
In Helsinki, you'll find tourist information offices at the
boat terminals, on the market square, and next to the
train station. They are uniformly friendly, very helpful,
well stocked in brochures, and blond. The best for our
purposes is the market square office (8:30-18:00, Saturday 8:30-13:00, closed Sunday, shorter hours off-season,
tel. 1693-757 or 174 088). Pick up the city map, the
"Route Map" (public transit), "Helsinki on Foot" (six
walking tours), the "Museums" brochure, the quarterly
"Helsinki Guide," with a great primer for the city's
architecture, and the youthful "Exploring Helsinki,"
which is loaded with answers to questions you should
have. Ask about the "3T" tourist tram and the city walking tours. Go over your sightseeing plans to be sure it'll all
work today. There is a free phone for local calls on the
wall. You can call 058 for recorded events and sights
hours in English any time.

Public Transit
With the "route map" and a little mental elbow grease,
you've got the city by the tail when you take advantage of
the buses and trams. Each ticket costs 6.50 mk, is good
for an hour of travel, and is purchased from the driver.
The "Helsinki Card"—free entry to city sights and use of
all buses and trams all day for 65 mk—isn't worthwhile
for our plans. It expires each midnight, not after 24
hours. The tourist tram, 3T, and its explanatory brochure
are worth a look.

Sightseeing Highlights
▲▲▲The Downtown Helsinki Walk—Harbor to
Train Station—The colorful and compact city center is
a great area to roam. Here are a few ideas on downtown
Helsinki:
   The Market Square, each day from 6:30 to 14:00 and
again from 15:30 to 20:00, is a colorful outdoor market at
the head of the harbor where the cruise ships dock.
Don't miss the busy two-tone red brick indoor market
hall adjacent. Across the street you'll see the City Tourist

Office. Drop in to check out the huge aerial photo of downtown and ask questions.

One block inland behind the Tourist Office are the fine neoclassical Senate Square and the Lutheran Cathedral. You'll pass the Schroder Sport Shop on Unioninkatu with a great selection of popular Finnish-made Rapula fishing lures—ideal for the fisherman on your gift list. Next to the Tourist Office step into the delightful "Jugendsalen." Designed, apparently, by a guy named Art Nouveau, this free and pleasant information center for locals offers interesting historical exhibits and a public W.C. The art deco interior is a knockout. (Open Monday-Friday 9:00-18:00, Sunday 12:00-18:00, closed Saturday, Pohjoisesplanadi 19.)

Across the street in the park facing the square is my favorite cafe in northern Europe, the Cafe Kappeli. When you've got some time, dip into this turn-of-the-century gazebolike oasis of coffee, pastry, and relaxation. Built in the nineteenth century, it was a popular hangout for local intellectuals and artists. Today the area closest to the market offers the romantic tourist waiting for his ship to sail a great 7 mk cup of coffee memory (or a reasonable light lunch).

Behind the cafe runs the park sandwiched between the north and south Esplande—Helsinki's top shopping boulevard. Walk it. The north (tourist office) side is most interesting for window shopping, people-watching, and sun-worshiping. You'll pass the Marimekko store, the huge Academic Bookstore, designed by Alvar Aalto, nearby at 1 Keskuskatu, which has a great map and travel guide section. Finally you'll come to the prestigious Stockman's department store—Finland's Harrod's and one of many that claim to be "Europe's largest." This best, oldest, and most expensive store in town has fine displays of local design. Just beyond is the main intersection in town, Esplande and Mannerheimintie. Nearby you'll see the famous "Four Smiths" statue. (They say, "If a virgin walks by, they'll strike the anvil." It doesn't work. I tried.)

A block to the right through a busy shopping center is the harsh (in a serene way) architecture of the central train station, designed by Saarinen in 1916. Wander around inside. Continuing past the "Hotelli keskus" room-finding office and the "Posti," past the statue, return to Mannerheimintie, which leads to the large white Finlandia Hall, another Aalto masterpiece. Normally it's not open, but ask at the TI about tours. Across the street is the excellent little Finnish National Museum (designed by Finland's first three great architects), and a few blocks behind that is the sit-down-and-wipe-a-tear beautiful rock church, Temppeliaukio. Sit, enjoy the music. It's a wonderful place to end this Welcome to Helsinki walk.

From nearby Arkadiankatu Street, bus #24 will take you to the Sibelius monument in a lovely park. The same ticket is good on a later #24. Ride to the end of the line—the bridge to the Seurasaari island and Finland's open-air folk museum. From here, ride bus #24 back to the Esplande.

▲▲▲**Orientation Tour**—A fast and very good 2-hour introductory tour leaves daily from both terminals immediately after the ships dock. The rapid-fire three-language tour costs 75 mk and gives a good historic overview, a look at all the important buildings from the Olympic Stadium to embassy row, with too-fast ten-minute stops at the Lutheran Cathedral, the Church in the Rock (Temppeliaukio), and Sibelius Monument. You'll learn strange facts like how they took down the highest steeple in town during World War II so the Soviets in Estonia, just 55 miles over the water, couldn't see their target. You'll also see where they filmed the Moscow Railway Station scenes in *Dr. Zhivago* (the low red brick building near the Viking Terminal). If you're on a tight budget and don't care to get the general overview of Helsinki, you can do the essence of this tour on your own as explained in my city walk (above). But I thoroughly enjoyed listening to the guide—he sounded like an audio shredder that was occasionally turned off so English could come out. They'll drop you off at the market square, near the

national museum (if you ask), or at your hotel by 11:30.
Similar tours also leave from downtown at 10:00 and
11:00, 2 ½ -hour tours are basically the same with a trip
out to the planned "garden city" suburb of Tapiola. There
is a shorter (no stop at Lutheran Cathedral), nearly as
good, cheaper tour (50 marks and included on the Helsinki card, tel. 585 166), but it starts at the train station. I
like the "pick you up at the boat and drop you at your
hotel or back on the market square" efficiency of the 9:30
tour. Buy your ticket on board or at the tourist desk in the
terminal (availability no problemi).

▲▲ **Lutheran Cathedral**—With its dominant green
dome overlooking the city and harbor, this church is the
masterpiece of Carl Ludwig Engel. Open the pew gate
and sit savoring neoclassical Nirvana. Finished in 1852,
the interior is pure architectural truth. Open 9:00 to
19:00, 12:00 to 18:00 on Sundays, until 17:00 in winter.
From the top of the steps, study Europe's finest neoclassical square. The Senate building is on your left. The small
blue stone building with the slanted Mansart roof in the
far left corner is from 1757, one of just two pre-Russian
conquest buildings remaining in Helsinki. On the right is
the University building. Czar Alexander II, a friend of Finland's, is honored by the statue in the square.

▲▲▲**Temppeliaukio Church**—Another great piece of
church architecture, this was blasted out of solid rock and
capped with a copper and skylight dome. It's normally
filled with recorded music and awestruck visitors. I
almost cried. Another form of simple truth, it's impossi-
ble to describe. Gawk upward at a 14-mile-long coil of
copper wire. Forget your camera, just sit in the middle,
ignore the crowds, and be thankful for peace (under your
feet is an air raid shelter that can accommodate 6,000
people). Open Monday through Saturday 10:00 to 20:00,
Sunday 12:00 to 14:00 and 19:00 to 20:00. To experience
the church in action, attend the Lutheran English service
(Sundays at 15:00, 14:00 in the off-season) or one of the
many concerts. You can buy individual slides or the picture book.

▲ **Sibelius Monument**—Hundreds of stainless steel pipes shimmer over a rock in a park to honor Finland's greatest composer. Bus #24 stops here (or look quickly from the bus) on its way to the open-air folk museum.

▲ **Seurasaari Open-Air Folk Museum**—Inspired by Stockholm's Skansen, also on a lovely island on the edge of town, this is a collection of 100 historic buildings gathered from every corner of Finland. Many of the buildings are staffed with an information person from 11:00 to 17:00. It's wonderfully furnished and gives us rushed visitors a great opportunity to sample the far reaches of Finland without even leaving the capital city. Buy the 10 mk guidebook. Off-season it's quiet, just you, log cabins, and birch trees, and almost not worth a look. 10 mk entry, open daily 11:00 to 17:00 from June through August; 9:30 to 15:00 Monday through Friday, 11:00 to 17:00 Saturday and Sunday in May and September. Ride bus #24 to the end of the line and walk across the quaint footbridge. The boat from downtown is overpriced. Call or check at the TI for tour and evening folk dance schedules (usually four nights a week, tel. 484712).

For a 10 mk bottomless cup of coffee in a cozy-like-someone's-home setting, stop by the Tamminiementien Kahvilia (near the Seurasaari bridge, up the road at Tamminiementie 8). Great bagels and Chopin, too.

▲▲ **National Museum**—A pleasant, easy to handle collection covering Finland's story from A-Z with good English descriptions in a grand building designed by three of Finland's greatest early architects. I enjoyed the neoclassical furniture, portraits of Russia's last czars around an impressive throne, the folk costumes, and the very well done Finno-Ugric exhibit downstairs (with a 20-page English guide to help explain the Finns, Estonians, Lapps, Hungarians, and their more obscure Finno-Ugric cousins). Open daily 11:00 to 16:00 and 18:00 to 21:00 Tuesdays, 10 mk, across the street from the Finlandia Hall, tel. 40251.

▲▲ **Uspensky Russian Orthodox Cathedral**—Hovering above the market square, blessing the harbor, is a fine icon experience (9:30-16:00, Monday-Friday).

▲ **Harbor tours**—Several boat companies line the market square offering 90-minute, 50 mk cruises around the waterfront nearly every hour. The narration is slow moving and in three languages, but if you're museumed out, tired of walking, and the weather's good, it's a good break.

▲ **Flea Market**—Hietalahti Market is Finland's biggest flea market (Monday-Saturday 8:00-14:00, summer evenings Monday-Friday, 15:30-20:00), well worth the 15-minute walk from the harbor.

Soumenlinna—The "fortified island" is a 20-minute ferry ride (15 mk round-trip, on the half-hour) from the market square. The old fort is now a popular park with several museums.

Sauna—Finland's vaporized fountain of youth is the sauna. Skip the hotel saunas for the more authentic (complete with birch twigs and local instruction on their use) public saunas. These cost around 20 mk and are listed in the "Exploring Helsinki" publication.

Tapiola—This futuristic planned community created a real stir in the '50s. It mixes residential and business districts with nature, keeping the pedestrian world unstressed by mindless motor traffic. Getting well worn and almost outgrowing its cuteness, it's still interesting. The 2½-hour city tours give it a quick drive-through. Frequent buses (9 mk, 15 minutes, a few miles out of town) give you a look without a tour.

Nightlife—Remember Finland was the first country to give their women the vote. The sexes are equal in the bars and on the dance floor, too. Finns are easily approachable and tourists are not a headache to the locals as they are in places like Paris and Munich. While it's easy to make friends, anything alcoholic is very expensive. Good bars to meet people are Adlon, Sky Bar, and Kaivohuone. For very cheap fun, Hietaranta beach is where the local kids hang out (even skinny dip) at 22:00 or 23:00. The city is one of Europe's safest after dark.

Accommodations

Helsinki is very expensive. The standard budget hotel double costs close to $100. But there are so many special

deals on dorm and hostel alternatives that you'll manage
easily. You have three basic budget options—cheap
youth hostels, student dorms turned "summer hotels," or
expensive business-class hotels at a special summer or
weekend clearance sale rate.

Summer (June 15-August 15) is "off-season" in Helsinki, as are weekends (Friday, Saturday, and Sunday). You
can safely arrive in the morning and expect to find a
budget room. Next to the train station (a pleasant 20-
minute walk from your boat, or tram 3B from Silja, bus
#13 from Viking, on arrival only) is the "Hotellcentralen"
room-finding service (Hotellikeskus). Open May to mid-
September from 9:00 to 21:00 (Saturday until 19:00, Sunday 10:00 until 18:00); off-season, 10:00 to 18:00 Monday
through Friday only. For 10 mk, they'll book you a room
in the price range of your choice. They know what wild
bargains are available on this first day of the rest of your
tour. Consider a luxury hotel clearance deal, which may
cost $20 more than the cheapies. Ask about any Helsinki
card "specials," which lower prices from mid-June to
early September and on weekends. Their 10 mk fee is reasonable, but they're happy to do the job over the phone
for free. Call up from the harbor (tel. 90/171133, Monday-
Friday 8:00-9:00).

Hostels: Kallion Retkeilymaja—Cozy, cheery, central, well run, and very cheap. Kitchen facilities, small
(only 30 beds); 40 mk for dorm bed (boys) or a bed in
5-bed rooms (girls). Closed 11:00-15:00. Open only June
through August. Porthaniankatu 2. Tel. 90/70992590.
From Market Square, take tram 1 or 2 to Hakaniemi
Square Market.

**Olympic Stadium Hostel (Stadionin Retkeilymaja,
IYHF)**—Big, crowded, impersonal, last resort bed. 45
mk, or 60 mk with no YH card. Open all year. Tel.
496071. Take tram 3T, 4, 7, or 10 to the Olympic Stadium.

Interpoint Youth Hostel (55 mk dorm beds,
Merikasarminkatu 3, tel. 169 3699) is another good
summer-only place in the city center.

Summer Hotels: These are central, modern, college
dorms put to good use as tourist hotels during the school

holidays (June, July, August). They offer the cheapest doubles in town, including breakfast, with saunas and budget cafeterias. **Academica Hotel** has 216 doubles, with private showers and toilets, 300 mk per double (June-August only). They also have a hostel section with cheap doubles (14 Hietaniemenkatu, tel. 440171, bus #18 or tram 3T). **Satakuntatalo Summerhotel** charges 250 mk/double (Lapinrinne 2A, tel. 6940311).

Classy "Real" Hotels: Hotel Anna is plush and very central (near Mannerheimintie and Esplanadi), a 15-minute walk from the boat. It is one of the best values in town with 500 mk doubles renting for 425 mk in the summer (1 Annankatu, tel. 648011). **Hotel Olympia** is not so central but on the T3 tram line. This is often about the least expensive hotel in town (400 mk doubles in the summer, 2 Lantinen Brahenkatu, tel. 750801).

Eating in Helsinki

Dining here is—you guessed it—expensive. But a good choice is worth the splurge. Most interesting is probably Russian food. Most popular, with meals for around 100 mk, are the **Kazbek Restaurant** (in the Olympia Hotel, great three-course Georgian meals, tel. 763 848), the **Troikka** (good Russian food in a tsarific setting, Caloniu-kesenkatu 3, tel. 445229 for reservations), and **Kassaka** (old Russian style, Meritullinkatu 13, tel. 1356-288).

The **Palace Cafe**, overlooking the harbor and market square above the Palace Hotel, is a good and not too exorbitant place for lunch. For a meal with folk music, ask at the tourist office about the dinner show at the Seurasaari Open-Air Folk Museum.

The best food values are, of course, the department store cafeterias and a picnic assembled from the colorful stalls on the harbor and the nearby bakery. Don't miss the red brick indoor market on the edge of the square. At the harbor you'll also find several local fast food stalls and delicious fresh fish (cooked if you like), explosive little red berries, and sweet carrots. While the open-air market is most fun, produce is cheaper in large grocery stores. Each open-air market has a popular-with-local-shoppers "tent cafe."

In the train station, you'll find the **Eliel** self-service restaurant and a 35 mk midday special.

An Extra Day—Turku and Nantali

It's tempting to spend a second day in Finland. Turku, the
historic old capital of Finland, is just a 2 ½ -hour train ride
from Helsinki (six times a day, 65 mk, the departure
shortly after noon works best, free with Eurail or save
50% by getting RR connection with boat ticket). The
medieval town of Nantali is an easy bus ride (30 minutes,
10 mk, 4 per hour) from Turku. Viking and Silja boats sail
each evening from Turku to Stockholm at 21:30 (and the
fare from here saves you enough money to pay for the
extra train ride).

Turku has a handicraft museum in a cluster of wooden
houses (the only part of town that survived a devastating
fire in the early 1800s), an impressive old cathedral, and a
busy market square.

Nearby Nantali is a well-preserved old wooden town
with a quaint harbor. These towns get good publicity, but
I found the side trip a little disappointing. The train ride
is nothing special, Turku (because of its fire) is a pale
shadow of Helsinki, and Nantali is cute, commercial, and
offers little if you've seen or will see Sigtuna near
Stockholm.

A Side Trip to Leningrad

It's easy to arrange an individual tour from Helsinki to
Leningrad (with no Intourist guide) through Finnsov
Tours (Eerikinkatu 3, 00100 Helsinki, tel. 90/694-2011,
ask for Kristina Mailander). You need about a month to
make arrangements from home. For around $400 you get
a round-trip Helsinki-Leningrad train ticket (first class)
and three nights in a simple hotel. The cheapest rooms
are available in the Olgino Campground caravans (to
Westerners by request only). With normal social skills, a
few Russian words, and a little luck, you can get invited to
the banquet room upstairs in the main hotel as the guest
of honor of Soviet citizens eager to eat, drink, and dance
with a new American friend.

UPPSALA TO OSLO

In some ways, Uppsala is more historic than Stockholm. Its cathedral and university win many "oldest, largest, tallest"-type awards, and the compact and bustling little city makes for a fine morning stop before the long drive across the green and wide open, but rather dull, spaces of Sweden to Oslo.

Suggested Schedule	
9:30	Dock in Stockholm, pick up your car, and drive to Uppsala.
10:30	Sightsee in Uppsala, enjoying the river-straddling old town, the historic cathedral, and the university flavor.
12:30	Picnic in the car as you drive, high-tailing it west to Oslo.
20:00	Arrive and set up in Oslo.

Transportation
From downtown Stockholm, signs direct you clearly to the E-4 highway and Uppsala, 40 miles to the north. Park as close to the twin cathedral spires as you can.

If you're going directly from Stockholm to Oslo, follow Sveavegen west and follow signs to E-3/E-4 south. Later you'll follow E-18.

From Uppsala to Oslo, it's about 325 miles; that's seven hours of mostly clear freeway motoring. Leaving Uppsala, follow signs for Route 55 and Norrkoping. When you hit E-18, just follow the Oslo signs past forests, lakes, and prettily painted wooden houses. It's very pleasant, but I'd stop only to fill and empty the tanks.

There are no border formalities unless you've got a tax refund to process for something you bought duty-free in Sweden. At the border, change money at the bank desk at the little tourist information kiosk (left-hand side of road, open 10:00-18:00 daily in summer, fair rates, 15 kr per traveler's check fee, pick up their free Oslo map and "What's On" publication). Call your Oslo hotel to report your progress and anticipated late arrival.

The ride from the border to Oslo is particularly scenic. The freeway butts you right up against downtown Oslo. Just follow the E-18 signs to "Sentrum," then "Sentral Stasjon" and "P-hus." If you're going directly to a room on the West end, follow signs to "Oslo V," veering right toward the palace immediately after passing the harbor-front. The TI and room-finding service is in the station. There's short-term parking, but you may want to deep-store your car in the safe, expensive, and most central garage. Look for the big blue "P" sign with a roof over it, 10 kr per hour, 110 kr per day.

Uppsala

Historic Uppsala's sights, along with its 30,000 students, cluster around the university and cathedral. Just over the river is the bustling shopping center and pedestrian zone. Its helpful tourist office has a branch near the cathedral (open until 19:00 in summer) and one in the castle (shorter hours). Off-season use the main office across the river near Stora Torget, tel. 018/117500 or 161825. Pick up their entertaining, helpful, and free Uppsala guide. The free and cute little Uppland Museum is on the river by the waterfall. Nearby is the Carl Linnaeus Garden and Museum and the sixteenth-century castle (with its slice of castle life exhibits) on the hilltop overlooking the town.

Sightseeing Highlights

▲▲**Uppsala Cathedral**—One of Scandinavia's largest and most historic cathedrals has a breathtaking interior, the tomb of King Gustavus Wasa, and twin 400-foot spires. Excellent tours leave several times daily (often in English, on polite request) in summer. Otherwise, push the English button, sit down, and listen to the tape-recorded introduction in the narthex opposite the tourist information table (open 8:00-20:00, daily June-August, until 18:00 off-season).

The University—Scandinavia's first university was

founded here in 1477. Carl von Linnaeus and Anders Celsius are two famous grads. Several of the old buildings are open to guests. A very historic but not much to see, old silver-bound Gothic Bible is on display with many other rare medieval books in the Carolina Rediviva (library). The anatomy theater in the Gustavianum is thought-provoking. Its only show was a human dissection.

Gamla Uppsala—Old Uppsala is rooted deeply in history but now almost entirely lost in the sod of centuries. You'll see several grass-covered ancient mounds marking the prehistoric center of Sweden, the historic (but rebuilt) church, and a colorful and touristy pub that serves mead—a fourteenth-century honey-and-hops wine—out of silver-plated old horns. A 30 kr horn serves a small group. It's fun if you like history and mead like I do. Look at the postcards of Gamla Uppsala's grassy mounds from downtown—that's all you'll see if you go out there. Easy by car, not worth the headache by bus (#24 to the end of the line).

Lunch in Uppsala?—Browse through the lively Saluhallen, the riverside indoor market in the shadow of the cathedral. You'll find great picnic stuff and pleasant cafes. This entire university district abounds with inexpensive eateries.

▲**Sigtuna**—Possibly Sweden's cutest town, Sigtuna is basically fluff. You'll see a medieval lane lined with colorful wooden tourist shops, a very pleasant tourist office with reading room, a cafe, a romantic park, a promenade along the lake, an old church, and some rune stones. The harborside cafe sells delicious waffles with whipped cream and strawberries. (Just one hour from Stockholm by train to Marsta and then bus to Sigtuna. Bus #883 leaves Sigtuna for Uppsala about every two hours. By car, leave Stockholm on the E-4 to Uppsala and take the clearly marked Sigtuna exit.)

Accommodations in Sweden

All across Sweden you'll see "Rum" and "Stuga" or "Stugor" signs. Those are cheap rooms in private homes or bungalow-type huts. The town of Arjang, just before the Norwegian border, is a good place to stop if you don't make it to Oslo. The Argang TI (tel. 0573/14136, open daily, 9:00-20:00, until 18:00 in off-season) can book you a private room (170 kr doubles). **Hotel Karl XII** offers the cheapest hotel beds (300 kr per double without breakfast, Sveavagen #22, near the marketplace, tel. 0573/10156). The main drag leads left from the freeway through the center of town and on to the huge local campground (Sommarvik Fritidscenter, 225 kr for four-bed no-sheets huts and good facilities, tel. 0573/12060).

There are no budget accommodations between the border and Oslo. It would be a shame to do the scenic drive from Arjang to Oslo in the dark.

Oslo
Situated at the head of the 60-mile-long Oslo fjord, sur-rounded by forests, and 500,000 people small, Oslo's charm doesn't stop there. Norway's largest city, capital, and cultural hub is a smorgasbord of historic sights, trees, art, and Nordic fun. The ancient city of Oslo became Christiania under the Danes. Only in 1924 did it get its old name back.

The city is easy to manage: nearly all its sights are clustered around the central "barbell" (Karl Johan Street with the Royal Palace on one end and the new train sta-tion on the other) or in the Bygdoy Park, a ten-minute ferry ride across the harbor.

Oslo lacks the coziness of Copenhagen and the monu-mental grandeur of Stockholm. But it offers an exciting two-day slate of sightseeing thrills, and it's user-friendly with a very energetic tourist office. Even though it's expensive, the organized visitor will leave feeling very good about the time and money spent here.

Tourist Office
Oslo has two very helpful tourist offices—one in the city hall (Monday-Saturday 8:30-18:00, Sunday 9:00-17:00, tel. 02/427170) and one in the central station (daily 8:00-23:00, tel. 02/171124). Be sure to pick up the free

city map/guide, the "Sporveiskart" transit map, the "What's On in Oslo" publication (for the most accurate listing of museum hours and special events), and the free annual Oslo Guide. They sell a 24-hour transit pass called the "Tourist Ticket" (40 kr) and the Oslo card (24 hours, 80 kr; 48 hours, 120 kr; or 72 hours, 150 kr), which gives you free use of all city public transit, the tourist train, entry to all sights, 50 percent off on city bus tours, free parking, many more discounts, and a handy handbook.

If you'll be using the buses and trains, get and use the free "Sporveiskart" transit map. Tickets are good for one hour of transfers and cost 13 kr, and the mini-card gives you 4 trips at a discount—available as you board (bus information, tel. 417030). The TI can recommend bike rental places (or try Ben Rustae Eike, 32 Oscarsgate, tel. 44 18 80).

The central train station is very efficient and helpful with a late-hours TI, a room-finding service, a late-hours bank (fair rates with the normal 15 kr per check fee), a supermarket (7:00-23:00 daily), and an Interrail Center (offering any young traveler with a train pass 10 kr showers, free bagagge racks, a bright and clean lounge, cheap snacks, and an information center).

Youth/Student/Vagabonds

"Use It" is a hardworking youth information center (open mid-June through September 11:00-19:00, Saturday and Sunday 12:00-16:00, five minutes from the station at Mollergate 1, entry on Grubbegate, near the cathedral, tel. 02/41 10 39) providing cheap deals on rooms, and discounts on budget eateries (such as 20% off at my recommended vegetarian restaurant) and evening spots. They are adjacent to the YMCA sleep-in (KFUM, see below) and sponsor a great, free Thursday folk evening.

Accommodations

Oslo is very expensive, and, unlike its sister Scandinavian capitals, its hostels are few and fill up quickly. The TI in the Central Station has a very hardworking room-finding service (Innkvartering) that can set you up in a private

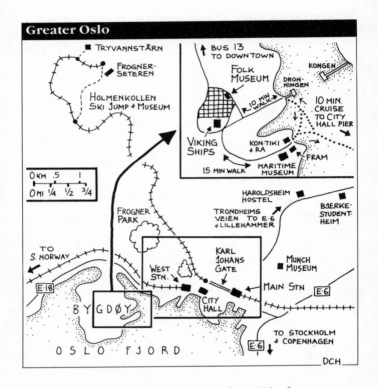

home (240 kr per double, no breakfast, 17 kr fee per person, at least two nights, normally not central) or sort through all the confusing hotel "specials" and get you about the best bed possible for your budget. July and early August are easy, but early June and September can be tight. The Innkvartering people are your advocates. They are notified each afternoon which hotels have dropped their prices to fill up, and they can find deals you'd never get on your own. You'll normally save money going with one of their clearance specials over what you'd pay going directly to the hotel on your own. In summertime Oslo, you'll generally sleep cheaper in hotels if you come into town without a reservation and use the TI. Always be clear about what you want (such as central, without shower, cheapest possible).

Budget Hotels Near the Station: Each of these places is within a two-minute walk of the station in a neighborhood your mom probably wouldn't want you hanging around in at night. The hotels themselves, however, are secure and comfortable. The only really safe place to park your car in this station area is in the park house (P-hus), handy but not cheap—110 kr per 24 hours.

City Hotel—This clean, basic, very homey place originated 100 years ago as a cheap place for Norwegians to sleep while they waited to sail to their new homes in America. Well run by the Salvation Army, its alcohol-free status earns it a special tax exemption that means cheaper rooms for us. Wonderful lounge. While this is the best of Oslo's cheap hotels, for the same money the TI can often get you a better summer discount hotel. 425-550 kr doubles with breakfast, Skippergatan 19, tel. 02/413610.

Hotel Fonix—Another basic, clean place, it lacks the City Hotel's comfyness but is a good value in Oslo. Doubles are 420-500 kr with breakfast, depending on plumbing, and a few small singles are available for 250 kr, Dronningensgt 19, tel. 02/425957.

Sjomannshjem—This "retired seaman's hotel" is one of Oslo's great bargains. Plain, clean, no-nonsense doubles cost only 280 kr; singles, 180 kr. A big breakfast is 30 kr extra. Some rooms include a shower. Tollbugt 4, 0152 Oslo, tel. 02/412005.

Other Budget Hotels: The **MS Hakon Jarl Hotel**, a refurbished steamer, retired after 30 years on the coastal run up to Nordkapp, is now permanently moored as central as you can be in Oslo—directly below the Akershus Fortress near the City Hall. 550 kr doubles in summer, otherwise a salty 700 to 800 kr splurge includes a lavish breakfast. Hotel guests get free and safe parking right on the dock. Nordre Akershus Kai, N-0150, Oslo, tel. 02/331606.

Standard Hotel is a good value normal hotel for 600 kr doubles with breakfast, but often rooms are as low as 350 kr through the TI or "Use It." Pilestredet 27, near the palace, tel. 02/203555. Another GVNH is the **Hotel Munch**. Rates are 600 kr doubles for 400 kr in summer. Munchsgate 5, tel. 02/424275. **Holtekilen Sommer-hotel** is a comfortable dorm 9 km from downtown. 300 kr doubles with breakfast. Tel. 02/533853.

Pensions and Hospits: Ellingsen's Pensjonat is run by a friendly lady whose name is Mrs. Wecking (you can pronounce it "Viking"). This is a textbook example of a good accommodations value with no lounge or break-fasts, dreary halls but fine rooms, fluffy down comforters, and a great location four blocks behind the Royal Palace (lots of 160 kr singles, three 260 kr doubles; call well in advance for doubles). Holtegt 25, 0355, Oslo 3, on the corner of Uranienborgveien and Holtegatan, near the Uranienborg church, it's #25 on the east side of the street, train #1 from the station, tel. 02/600359.

Cochs Pensjonat, which has plain rooms and stale wet-noodle atmosphere but is right behind the palace (train 11 to Parkveien 25, tel. 02/604836), and **Lindes Pensjonat** (near Frogner Park, train #2 to 41 Thomas Heftyes Gate, near Frogner Park, tel. 02/553282) are nothing special. But they have doubles for around 360 kr and offer access to the laundry room.

Youth Hostels: Haraldsheim Youth Hostel (IYHF), Oslo's huge, modern, well-run hostel, is open all year, situated far from the center on a hill with a grand view, and has a laundry and self-service kitchen. Its 270 beds (6 to a room) are often completely booked. (135 kr, with breakfast, 4 Haraldsheimveien, tram #1 or #7 from station to Sinsen, 4 km out of town, end of the line, tel. 02/155043. Call in the morning for a bed; they'll hold it until 18:00.)

Pan Hostel (IYHF) has 49 doubles, 7 triples, a super-market, a laundry, and a cafeteria and is peacefully located in a forest near a beach (132 kr per bed, Sogns-veien 218, 15 minutes on train #13 to Kringsja, tel. 02/237640).

Oslo Interpoint (YMCA, YWCA)—Located near the station, this sleep-in offers the cheapest mattresses in town with a fun but rugged atmosphere (70 kr, BYO

sleeping bag, open July through mid-August, Mollergate
1, entry from Grubbegate, look for KFUM sign, one block
beyond the cathedral, tel. 02/411039).

Food in Oslo

The thought of a simple open face sandwich (which
looks and tastes like half of something I can make, with
an inedible garnish added) for $5, and a beer for nearly as
much, ruins my appetite. Nevertheless, one can't continue to sightsee on postcards and train tickets alone.

My strategy is to splurge for a hotel that includes breakfast. A Norwegian breakfast is fit for a Viking (and any
Viking could zip-lock away a light lunch).

Have a picnic for lunch. There are plenty of grocery
stores (Rimi, on Rosenkrantzgate, just off the harbor
between the city hall and the castle, has great prices, and
the train station has a late-hours grocery) and picturesque
spots to give your feast some atmosphere. Don't forget a
tin full of fresh shrimp cooked and ready to eat from one
of the fishermen moored at the harbor.

Downtown Budget Meals: I eat dinner at a cafeteria.
(Since Norwegians eat early, between 16:00 and 19:00,
the cheapest places close by 19:00. Later dinners are elegant dining and normally quite expensive.) Pizzerias and
salad bars are the new trend. You'll find them near any
hotel—ask your receptionist for advice. Many pizzerias
have all-you-can-eat specials. Try **Den Roede Moelle** at
9 Brugata.

The **Aker Brygge** (harborfront mall) development has
some cheery cafes, classy delis, and open-till-22:00
restaurants and markets. Chinese and ethnic places are
everywhere and reasonable.

Oslo's several **Kaffistova cafeterias** are alcohol-free
and clean (check out the revolving toilet seats) and serve
simple, hearty, and typically Norwegian (read "bland")
meals for the best price around. At 8 Rosenkrantzgate,
you'll get your choice of an entrée and all the salad,
cooked vegetables, and "flat bread" you want (or at least
need) for around 50 kr at lunch (11:00-14:00) and 80 kr at

dinner. It's open from 11:00-22:00 (19:00 Saturday and 20:00 Sunday) in summer and closes earlier off-season. The **Torgstova Kaffistova** (13 Karl Johans Gate) closes at 18:00. Other cafeterias are found in department stores. The **Norrona Cafeteria** (central at 19 Grenson) is another budget-saver that closes at 18:00. Near the cathedral, **Mollers Kafe** (discount from "Use It", Marlboesgate 9) serves some of Oslo's cheapest decent meals.

Vegeta Vertshus, which has been keeping Oslo vegetarians fat and happily low on the food chain for 50 years, serves a huge selection of hearty vegetarian food that would satisfy even a Republican president. Fill your plate once for 65 kr or eternally for 95 kr. One plate did me fine. It's even cheaper à la carte (daily 10:00-23:00, no smoking, no alcohol, Munkedamsveien 3B, near top of Stortingsgata between palace and city hall, tel. 834232).

Behind the palace, near recommended Ellingsen Pension is the friendly and untouristy **B12 Cafe** (Bogstadveien 12, tel. 692273), which offers a fine daily special and cheap beer. The Greek cook sneaks out to see if all his food is being eaten.

Of course, there are plenty of wonderful and atmospheric ways to dine in Oslo, but most are expensive.

At Holmenkollen Ski Jump, the **Frognerseteren Hovedrestaurant** (tel. 143736) is a traditional, lavishly decorated Norwegian lodge perched high above Oslo. The house specialties are game—reindeer, elk, chuckers, pheasant—apple cake, and fallen ski jumpers. You'll find it under the big flagpoles, a short hike up from the ski jump. Forget the restaurant. The self-service cafeteria, inside or on the terrace, has fine dinners for under 100 kr—same chef, same kitchen, same view. Call for reservations. Open late. Take subway 15 and ask for directions. The last return trip is after midnight; there are three rides per hour.

Back downtown, the ritzy **Plaza Hotel** has a good value Dagens ratt (80 kr) lunch or dinner. And for a memorable splurge at Bygdoy (150 kr lunch), eat at the **Najaden Restaurant**.

OSLO

Sights of the Viking spirit—past and present—tell a thrilling story. Day 11 includes looks at the remains of ancient
Viking ships and more peaceful but equally gutsy modern boats like the *Kon Tiki, Ra*, and *Fram*. Then you'll
hear stirring stories of the local World War II Nazi resistance and trace the country's folk culture at the Norwegian
Open-Air Folk Museum.

Oslo is the smallest and probably least earthshaking of
the Nordic capitals. But brisk and almost brittle little Oslo
offers many more sightseeing thrills than you would
expect. On Day 12, you'll get a feel for the modern town
as you browse through the new yuppie-style harbor
shopping complex, touring Oslo's avante-garde city hall,
getting a good dose of Gustav Vigeland's sculpture, and
riding the scenic commuter train to the towering Holmenkollen ski jump and ski museum.

Suggested Schedule	Day 11
9:00	Visit the TI to confirm sightseeing plans, pick up maps and other information.
10:00	Tour Nazi Resistance Museum at Akershus Castle.
11:00	Guided tour of Akershus Castle. Explore ramparts and harbor view.
12:00	Buy picnic (Rimi grocery store two blocks west of city hall, shrimp from boats at harbor), catch ferry to Bygdoy, and eat with a city harbor view in the park near the museums.
13:30	Tour Fram and Kon Tiki museums. Walk to Viking ships (15 minutes).
15:30	Tour Viking Ships Museum.
16:00	Tour Open-Air Folk Museum (ask about any crafts demonstrations or folk music scheduled). Bus #30 or boat home.

Suggested Schedule Day 12	
10:00	City Hall Tour.
11:00	Free time to browse and stroll in city center, Aker Brygge (new "Festival Market" mall on the harbor) and walk Karl Johans Gate from palace to station.
16:00	Visit Vigeland Park, then see Vigeland Museum.
18:00	Subway to Holmenkollen, climb the ski jump for city view, tour ski museum and climb into the simulator. Stoke your appetite further with a hike up to the traditional Norsk dinner and a great sunset at Frognerseteren Hovedrestaurant, or return downtown for cheap Koffistova dinner.

Sightseeing Highlights

▲▲▲**Bygdoy**—This exciting cluster of sights is on a pleasant peninsula just across the harbor from downtown. The museums listed below are reached by bus #30 from the National Theater or by a special little ferry. The bus to Bygdoynes (13 kr, ticket good for one hour) leaves from City Hall or Radhuset every half hour, 8:30-21:00. The folk museum and Viking ships are near the first stop; the other museums are at the second stop, Bygdoynes. In the summer, a shuttle bus connects these sights. Otherwise, all four listed below are within a 15-minute walk of each other.

▲▲**Norwegian Folk Museum**—140 buildings brought from all corners of Norway are reassembled on these 35 acres. While Stockholm's Skansen claims to be the first (and was the first open to the public), this museum is a bit older, starting in 1885 as the king's private collection. You'll find craftspeople doing their traditional things, security guards disguised in cute, colorful, traditional local costumes, endless creative ways to make do in a primitive log-cabin-and-goats-on-the-roof age, a twelfth-century stave church, as well as a museum filled with toys and fine folk costumes. The place hops in the summer but is quite dead off-season. Try to catch the free one-hour guided walks (June-July Monday-Friday 13:00, Saturday and Sunday 14:00). Otherwise glean information from the 18 kr guidebook and the informative guards who look like Rebecca Boone's Norwegian pen pals. Open mid-May through August daily from 10:00 to 18:00; off-season, 11:00-16:00; Sundays, it opens an hour late. 35 kr. Ask about the folk dance performances, usually summer Sundays (for tour and dance and crafts demonstarations schedules, call 437020).

▲▲**Viking ships**—Three great ninth-century Viking ships and plenty of artifacts from the days of rape, pillage, and—ya sure betcha—plunder. Don't miss the old cloth and embroidery in the dark room you turn on by simply stepping into. There are no museum tours, but it's hard not to hear the bus tour guides explaining things to their English-speaking groups. There was a time when much of a frightened Europe closed every prayer with "and deliver us from the Vikings, Amen." Gazing up at the prow of one of these sleek time-stained vessels, you can almost hear the screams and smell the armpits of those redheads on the rampage (10:00-18:00 daily in summer, less in the off-season, 10 kr).

▲▲▲**The Fram**—This great ship took modern-day Vikings Amundsen and Nansen deep into the Arctic and Antarctic, farther north and south than any ship before. For three years the *Fram* was part of an arctic ice drift. The exhibit is fascinating. Read the ground floor displays, then explore the boat (10:00-17:45 daily in summer, 11:00-14:45 daily off-season, 10 kr).

▲▲**The Kon Tiki Museum**—Next to the *Fram* are the *Kon Tiki* and the *Ra II*, the boats Thor Heyerdahl built and sailed, 4,000 and 3,000 miles, respectively, to prove early South Americans could have sailed to Polynesia and Africans could have populated Barbados. He made enough money from his adventures to also prove that rich Norwegians can only stay that way by moving to low-tax Monaco (10:00-18:00 daily, 10:30-17:00 off-season, 12 kr).

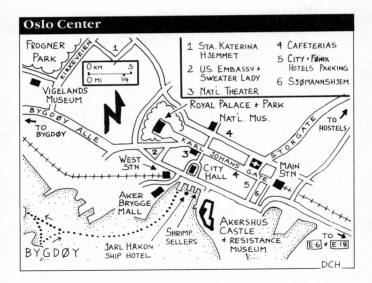

Oslo Center

FROGNER PARK
KIRKEVEIEN
VIGELANDS MUSEUM
BYGDØY ALLE
TO BYGDØY
WEST STN
AKER BRYGGE MALL
JARL HAKON SHIP HOTEL
SHRIMP SELLERS
BYGDØY

ROYAL PALACE + PARK
NAT'L. MUS.
KARL JOHANS GATE
CITY HALL
STORGATE
MAIN STN
AKERSHUS CASTLE + RESISTANCE MUSEUM
TO HOSTELS
TO E·6 + E·18

1 STA. KATERINA HJEMMET
2 U.S. EMBASSY + SWEATER LADY
3 NAT'L. THEATER
4 CAFETERIAS
5 CITY + FØNIX HOTELS PARKING
6 SJØMANNSHJEM

0 KM 5
0 MI ¼

DCH

▲**Norwegian Maritime Museum**—Next to the *Fram*, this museum provides a fine look at the maritime heritage of this very seafaring land. If you like the sea, this is a salt-lick. (Daily 10:00-20:00, off-season 10:30-16:00. 15 kr.)

Downtown Sights

▲▲**City Hall**—Oslo's richly decorated "Radhuset" was built in 1950 to celebrate her 950th birthday. Norway's leading artists all contributed to what was an avant-garde thrill in its day. The interior's 2,000 square yards of bold and colorful murals take you on a voyage through the collective psyche of Norway, from its simple rural beginnings through the scar tissue of the Nazi occupation and beyond. Guided tours, given free at 10:00, 12:00, and 14:00 Monday through Friday, make the place meaningful. Entry is on the Karl Johan side (the tourist office is on the harbor side). Open Monday through Saturday 10:00 to 15:00, Sunday 12:00 to 15:00. No admission charge.

▲**Akershus Castle**—One of the oldest buildings in town, this castle overlooking Oslo's harbor is mediocre by European standards but worth a look. Its grounds make a pleasant park with grassy ramparts, pigeon-roost

cannons, and great picnic spots and city views. Tours of
the interior (free; daily in summer at 11:00, 13:00, and
15:00, Sunday 13:00 and 15:00 only, 50 minutes long) are
interesting. Without a tour, you can read the English
information sheets in each room. Open daily from 10:00
to 16:00, Sunday from 12:30 to 16:00, May to mid-
September. Open Sundays only in the off-season. 10 kr.

▲▲ **Norwegian Resistance Museum**—A stirring story
about the Nazi invasion and occupation is told with wonderful English descriptions. This is the best look in
Europe at how national spirit can endure total occupation
by a foreign power. Located in the Akershus Castle. Open
daily in summer from 10:00 to 16:00, Sunday from 11:00
to 16:00. Closing is one hour earlier in the off-season. 10 kr.

▲ **National Gallery**—Located right downtown (13
Universitets Gata), this easy-to-handle museum is nothing earthshaking, but if you're into art it's worth a look
for its impressionist collection, its romantic Norwegian
art, and a roomful of Munch paintings. Open Monday,
Wednesday, Friday, and Saturday from 10:00 to 16:00,
Thursday from 10:00 to 20:00, Sunday from 11:00 to
15:00, and closed Tuesdays. Free.

▲▲ **Browsing**—Oslo's pulse is best felt along the central
Karl Johans Gate (from station to palace) and in the
trendy new harborside Aker Brygge Festival Market Mall
(a glass-and-chrome collection of sharp cafes and
polished produce stalls just west of the city hall).

▲▲▲**Vigeland Sculptures, Frogner Park and
Vigeland Museum**—The 75-acre park contains a lifetime of work by Norway's greatest sculptor, Gustav
Vigeland. One hundred seventy-five bronze and granite
statues—all nude and each one unique—surround the
60-foot-high tangled tower of 121 bodies called "the
monolith of life." The small blue "Guide to the Vigeland
Park" booklet is worthwhile. The park is more than great
art. It's a city at play. Enjoy its urban Norwegian
ambience. Then visit the wonderful Vigeland Museum to
see the models for the statues and much more in the
artist's studio. Don't miss the photos on the wall showing

the construction of the monolith. The museum is open daily from 10:00 to 18:00, Sunday from 12:00 to 19:00, closed Monday, 20 kr. Off-season, it's free but only open 12:00-16:00. The park itself is always free and open. Take train #2 or bus #72, #73, or #20 to Frogner Plass.

▲▲ **Edvard Munch Museum**—The only Norwegian painter to have a serious impact on European art, Munch is a surprise to many who visit this fine museum. His emotional, disturbing, and powerfully expressionist art is arranged chronologically: paintings, drawings, lithographs, and photographs by a strange and perplexing man. Don't miss *The Scream*, which captures the fright many feel as the human "race" does just that. Open Tuesday through Saturday from 10:00 to 20:00, Sunday from 12:00 to 20:00; off-season closed at 16:00 and all day Monday. 20 kr.

▲▲ **Holmenkollen Ski Jump and Ski Museum**—Just out of town is a tremendous ski jump with a unique museum of skiing. A pleasant subway ride (to Holmenkollen) gets you out of the city and into the hills and forests that surround Oslo. Ride the elevator and climb the 100-step stairway to the thrilling top of the jump for the best possible view of Oslo—and a chance to stand looking down the long and frightening ramp that has sent so many tumbling into the agony of defeat. The ski museum is a must for skiers—tracing the evolution of the sport from 4,000-year-old rock paintings to crude 1,500-year-old skis to the slick and quickly evolving skis of our century. (The Ski Jump and Museum are open daily from 9:00 or 10:00 to 22:00 in July, 20:00 in August, earlier closing off-season. 20 kr each or 30 kr together.)

For a special thrill, step into the "Simulator" and fly down the French Alps in a Disneyland-style downhill ski race simulator. My legs were exhausted after the 3 ½ - minute terror. This simulator, parked in front of the ski museum, costs 20 kr. (Japanese tourists wig over this one and are usually given a free ride after paying for four.)

A few more stops to the end of the subway line (Frognersetern) is the "Tryvannstarnet" observatory tower, offering a lofty 360-degree view with Oslo in the distance, the fjord and endless forests, lakes and soft hills. It's impressive but not necessary if you climbed the ski jump, which shows you Oslo much better.

▲▲**Folk Entertainment**— A group of amateur musicians and dancers gives a short, sweet, caring, and vibrant one-hour show (70 kr, 40 kr for students, each summer Monday and Thursday at 21:00, at the Oslo Concert Hall, the big brown glassy overpass on Monkedamsveien, tel. 833200; the recommended Vegata Vertshus restaurant is just up the street). Students should take advantage of the Interpoint/Use It-sponsored Thursday Norsk Folk evening. It's free at 20:00 with music, dancing, food, and lots of potential friends. (At Oslo Interpoint near the cathedral at Mollergate 1.)

Evenings—They used to tell people who asked about nightlife in Oslo that Copenhagen was only an hour away by airplane. Now Oslo has sprouted a nightlife of its own. The scene is always changing. The tourist office has information on Oslo's many cafes, discos, and jazz clubs. "Use It" has discount coupons to several hot spots.

Pools and Wet Fun—Oslo offers lots of water fun for about 30 kr. **Toyenbadet** (free with Oslo Card, open mid-May through mid-August, 7:00-19:00, Saturday and Sunday 10:00-17:00, Helgengate 90, 10 minutes walk from Munch Museum, tel. 671887) is a modern pool complex with mini golf and a 100-yard-long water slide. In Frogner Park, the **Frognerbadet** (May-August, Middelthunsgate 28, tel. 447429) has a sauna, pools, cafeteria, and high dives.

Shopping—For a good selection (but high prices) in sweaters and other Norwegian crafts, shop at Husfliden (Den Norske Husflidsforening, 4 Mollergate behind the cathedral, daily 9:00-17:00, Saturday until 14:00, tel. 421075), the retail center for the Norwegian Association of Home Arts and Crafts.

Shops are generally open from 9:00 to 17:00 (or 16:00 in summer). Many stay open until 19:00 on Thursdays and close early on Saturday and completely on Sunday.

LILLEHAMMER AND GUDBRANDSDALEN, NORWAY'S HEARTLAND

Drive north from Oslo, passing the Norwegian Philadelphia, Eidsvoll, where Norway's constitution was hammered out and signed. Then, after a picnic and tour through Norway's best folk museum at Maihaugen near Lillehammer, venture up the romantic Gudbrandsdal Valley—Peer Gynt country. Our destination is Jotunheim (the giant's home), land of Norway's most staggering mountains and Europe's biggest glacier.

Suggested Schedule

8:00	Drive out of Oslo, pass Eidsvoll (after an hour) and motor along Norway's largest lake to Lillehammer.
11:00	Catch the 11:00 walking tour through the traditional buildings and homes of this part of Norway in the Maihaugen open-air folk museum.
13:00	Picnic at museum.
14:00	Drive up scenic Gudbrandsdal Valley, stop at Lom church.
18:00	Check into hotel.

Transportation

It's three hours from Oslo to Lillehammer and four hours after that to Lom. Wind out of Oslo following signs for "E-26, Trondheim." In a few minutes, you're in the wide open pastoral countryside of eastern Norway. Norway's Constitution Hall is a five-minute detour off E-6 a couple of miles south of Eidsvoll in Eidsvoll Verk (follow the signs to Eidsvoll Bygningen). Then E-6 takes you along Norway's largest lake, Mjosa, through the town of Hamar, over a toll bridge (15 kr), and past more nice lake scenery into Lillehammer, site of the 1994 Winter Olympics. Signs direct you uphill from downtown Lillehammer to the Maihaugen museum. There's free parking near the pay lot

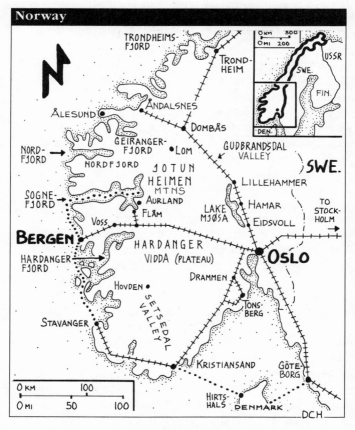

above the entrance. Then E-6 enters the valley of Gudbrandsdalen. From Lillehammar, cross the bridge again
and follow signs to E-6/Trondheim. At Otta, exit for Lom.

Sightseeing Highlights

▲**Eidsvoll Manor**—During the Napoleonic period,
Denmark was about to give Norway to Sweden. This ruf-
fled the patriotic feathers of Norway's Thomas Jeffersons
and Ben Franklins, and in 1814, Norway's constitution
was written and signed in this stately mansion. It's full of
elegant furnishings and stirring history—well worth a
stop and 5 kr (if you're driving). The friendly ticket lady

is a source of information, and there's a good guidebook. Open daily from 10:00 to 17:00, 12:00 to 14:00 off-season. Unfortunately, if you're following today's suggested schedule, you'll have to skip this.

▲▲▲**Maihaugen Open-Air Folk Museum**—Founded by a "visionary dentist" around the turn of the century, this wonderfully laid out look at the local culture gets my "we try hardest" award. Dr. Anders Sandvig started the collection in 1887. With 130 old buildings from the Gudbrandsdalen region and a fascinating indoor museum showing the interior of the shops of 60 crafts- and tradespeople (such as a hatter, cooper, bookbinder, and Dr. Sandvig's old dental office), this provides a great introduction to the long and traditional valley you are entering. In summer the museum bustles with weaving and baking activities. There's a thorough English guidebook (48 kr), English descriptions at each house, and loving (and free) 45-minute guided tours daily in English at 11:00, 13:00, and 15:00 (and sometimes on request).

The museum welcomes picnickers and has a good cafe and an outdoor restaurant. 35 kr entry. Open daily from 9:00 to 19:00 June through August, 10:00 to 16:00 shoulder season, 11:00 to 14:00 from September 15 through May 15 (tel. 062/50135—call to be sure you arrive for a tour, especially outside of summer). Ask on arrival about special events, crafts, or music, and don't miss the indoor museum. (Steep 20-minute walk up from the train station, or take the bus to the Nybu hospital.)

▲**Lillehammer**—This pleasant winter and summer resort town has a happy old wooden pedestrian zone and several interesting museums including a popular transportation museum. But its Maihaugen Open-Air Folk Museum is our reason to stop here. This small-time town will one way or another (locals figure it'll take Swedish money) become big time as the 1994 Olympics approach. As of late 1990, Lillehammer had designed 1994 Olympics sweatshirts and that was about all. Lillehammer's TI is open from 9:00 to 20:00, less on weekends and off-season (tel. 062/59 299).

As you drive north of town, you'll see two goofy kids' sights. Just past the dam, over the river, a huge 40-foot-tall green troll, the entry to a children's park (you walk under his legs) with 50 rides and activities associated with Norwegian fairy tales. It's a favorite with local children (expensive at 85 kr, open 10:00-19:00 June 15 to September 15, tel. 062/74 222). Farther up the road, on your right this time, you'll pass "Lilleputthammer," a ¼ -size downtown Lillehammer (20 kr, half price for very short people, open 10:00-19:00, mid-June to mid-August, tel. 062/78 335). If you're still kidding around, Vannland (Waterland) is a nearby water park.

▲**Gudbrandsdalen**—This "Queen of Valleys" has connected north and south Norway since ancient times. You'll pass time-worn hills, velvet farms, and lots of riverside campgrounds. This is Peer Gynt country, and two scenic side trips give visitors a good dose of the wild beauty associated with this Norwegian Huck Finn.

Peer Gyntveien is a 30 kr troll road that leaves E-6 at Tretten, looping west for 25 miles and rejoining E-6 at Vinstra. This trip sounds romantic, but it's basically a windy, windy dirt road over a high desolate heath and scrub brush plateau with fine mountain views: scenic, but so is E-6. The second, lesser known but more rewarding scenic side trip is the Peer Gynt Setervei. For another toll you'll loop east from E-6 from Vinstra (at the Texaco station) to Kvam via Rondablikk, climbing to 3,650 feet and passing very close to old Peer Gynt's farm. (If you do this 25-mile detour, pick up the little green Peer Gynt booklet that tells his legend and describes the drive.)

▲ **Lom**—This isn't much of a town—except for its great stave church, which causes the closest thing to a tour bus jam this neck of the Norwegian woods will ever see. Drop by the church (you'll see its dark spire just over the bridge, free, open 9:00-21:00 daily mid-June through mid-August, shorter off-season, fine 3 kr leaflet), and take advantage of the tourist information office (9:00-21:00 daily in summer, shorter hours Monday-Friday only off-season, tel. 062/11286) before leaving Route 15 for Route 55. Lom has plenty of accommodations (TI can arrange), but I'd sleep elsewhere.

Accommodations

I've listed a variety of places here stretching from Kvam to
Boverdal, past Lom, depending on your style, budget,
and speed. This is a very popular vacation valley for Norwegians, and you'll find loads of reasonable small hotels
and campsites with huts (*hytter* means bungalow, *rom* is
private room, and *ledig* means not full) for those who
aren't quite campers. These huts normally cost around
170 kr and can take from 4 to 6 people. They are popular
and often filled in July. Although they are simple, you'll
have a kitchenette and access to a good W.C. and shower.
When available, sheets rent for an extra 40 kr per person.
Local TIs can find you rooms. Only in the middle three
weeks of July will finding a bed without a reservation
require any luck.

   Kvam (two hours from Lillehammer): The **Kirketei-
gen Ungdomssenter**, literally "Church Youth Center,"
just behind the Old Kvam church is run by friendly
Katrina and Hakon Olsen, who welcome travelers like us
all year long. They have camping places (40 kr per tent or
van), huts (170 kr per four-person hut), and very simple
4-bed rooms (170 kr per room). They also have a rustic
old chalet near Rondablikk in Peer Gynt country. Sheets
(40 kr) and blankets (10 kr) can be rented. I stayed in a
very old sod-roofed log cabin hut and enjoyed fine clean
facilities. (2650 Kvam i. Gudbrandsdalen, turn right just
before the town church, tel. 062/940, call in advance).
One hundred meters away is the **Sinclair Vertshuset
Motel**, Cafeteria, Pizzeria (basic doubles without
personality—about 450 kr June-August, cheaper off-
season, good cheap pizzas, tel. 062/94024), named after a
Scotsman who led a band of adventurers into this valley
attempting to set up their own Scottish kingdom. They
failed (and were all kilt).

   Roisheim (three-hour drive from Lillehammer, ten
minutes past Lom), in a marvelously remote mountain
setting, is a storybook hotel comprised of a cluster of
centuries-old sod-roofed log farmhouses. Filled with
antiques, Norwegian travelers, and friendliness by its

industrious owners, Unni and Wilfried Reinschmidt, Roisheim is a cultural end in itself. Each room is rustic but elegant with doubles from 450 to 600 kr. Some are in old log huts with low ceilings and heavy beams. The honeymooners' special has a canopy bed. Wilfried, a well-known chef, serves memorable meals. Gilded lily breakfasts are 80 kr, and a full three-course traditional dinner, one Norway's royalty travels far to eat, is served at 19:00 (210 kr, call ahead so they'll be prepared). Arrive early enough to enjoy the living room, library, old piano, and a peaceful walk—a very memorable splurge. Look around for living bits of the history you learned at Maihaugen—the chef ringing the dinner bell, the comb box in the dining room, what else?

Wilfried, a German who married the Norwegian Unni (when they worked on the Norwegian American cruise line), gives guests a nightly, after-dinner tour of his historic domain. Open April through mid-October, 6 miles south of Lom on the Sognefjell Road (55) in Boverdalen, tel. 062/12031, fax 062/12151. Nobody's home November through January.

Old World romantic, like Roisheim, but cheaper and much less impressed with itself is the **Elvesaeter Hotel**. (420 kr doubles, including breakfast; 350 kr for doubles in the annex; 110 kr dinners). Open June through late September. It's about ten minutes farther up road 55, past Boverdal, tel. 062/12000.

Boverdalen youth hostel, just a couple of miles from Roisheim and in another galaxy pricewise (4- to 8-bed rooms, 65 kr per bed, doubles for 160 kr, hot and self-serve meals, open mid-May through September, tel. 062/12064) is the center of the last little community (store, post office, campground, toll road up to Galdhopiggen area) you'll pass before entering the Jotunheim high country. The nearby **Sjoa hostel** (tel. 062/360037) is nowhere near as handy.

JOTUNHEIM COUNTRY—THE GIANT'S HOME

Drive over Norway's highest mountain pass, deep into Jotunheim (the "giant's home") country. Norway's highest road takes you past her highest mountains. Then do the white knuckle corkscrew road down to the head of Norway's longest fjord before climbing back up to a slow but fierce tongue of Europe's biggest glacier, where a local expert will take you on a guided 2-hour glacier walk. You can make it restful, spending the night in tiny Solvorn on the Sognafjord, or push it by catching the ferry across the fjord and driving over the remote and exciting Lardal pass into the most beautiful fjord in Norway, Aurland's fjord, a branch of the Sognafjord. A superlative day—the most superlative day ever.

Suggested Schedule	
9:00	Easy morning exploring Norway's highest mountain road.
12:00	Hike to Nigardsbreen glacier for a picnic on ice.
17:40	Catch ferry from Kaupanger to Aurland, or get out at Revnes and drive over Lardal to Aurland. (Note: this is a very long—some would argue impossible—day. It's important to be in Aurland to catch the once-a-day morning ferry to Gudvangen. To make it easier, skip the glacier side trip, or sleep before Kaupanger and ferry just about as beautifully from Kaupanger to Gudvangen tomorrow.)

Sightseeing Highlights
Norwegian Geology Lesson—The Scandinavian peninsula is a ramp sloping up from flat Finland and eastern Sweden to the 8,000-foot peaks in the west of Norway.

Then, in a tangle of deep and narrow fjords, the landmass plunges back to sea level on the rugged west coast.

The region enjoys very mild weather for its latitude today thanks to the warm Gulf Stream. But 3 million years ago, an ice age made this land as inhabitable as the center of Greenland. Slowly the ice receded. The Danes say that while their highest point is only 600 feet, the glaciers dragged all of Norway's best topsoil to them.

As the last glaciers of the ice age cut their way to the sea, they grooved out long troughs—today's fjords. Since the ice was thicker inland and only a relatively thin lip at the coast, the gouging was deeper inland. The average fjord is 4,000 feet deep far inland and only around 600 feet deep where it reaches the open sea.

▲**Jotunheim**—Norway's highest mountain is Gald-hopiggen. The Boverdal/Roisheim area is a popular jumping-off point for hikes to the 8,000-foot summit and guided glacier walks in the summer. From Roisheim, you can drive 18 km to Spiterstulen mountain hotel/lodge where Galdhopiggen is a 4-hour hike up and a 2-hour hike down. Nearby are daily guided glacier hikes. From the Juvass hutta, there are 5-hour guided hikes to the summit and back daily at 10:00 in the summer. Get specifics on this locally.

▲▲**Sognefjell**—Norway's highest mountain crossing (4,600 feet at the summit) is a thrilling drive through a can-can line of northern Europe's highest mountains. In previous centuries, the farmers of Gudbrandsdalen took their horse caravans over this difficult mountain pass on their necessary treks to Bergen. Just a shade more comfortably, you'll follow the same route. Today the road (Route 15), still narrow and windy, is usually closed from mid-October through May. The descent from Sognefjell, with ten hairpin turns between Turtagro and Fortun, is an exciting finale. Be sure to stop, get out, and enjoy the lavish views. Enjoy each turn to its fullest; it may be your last. (Mountain driving tips: use low gears and lots of patience both up, to keep it cool, and down, to save your brakes. Uphill traffic gets the right-of-way, but drivers, up

or down, considerately dive for the nearest fat part whenever they meet. Ask back seat drivers not to scream until
you've actually been hit or left the road.)

▲**Lusterfjorden**—After the mountains you'll drive
along an arm of the famous Sognefjord called Lusterfjord.
This is still rugged country. Only 2% of the land here is
fit to build or farm on. At Nes, look back at the impressive
Feigumfoss Waterfall. Drops and dribbles come from
miles around for this 200-yard tumble.

In Dale, the thirteenth-century stone Gothic church
with fourteenth-century frescoes is unique and worth a
peek. Just off the road on the fjord is the tiny town of
Marifjora which has a lefse bakery in action (Monday-
Friday 9:00-16:00, the traditional doughy potato bread,
or lefsa, is on sale).

▲▲**Urnes Stave Church**—From the peaceful Victorian
village of Solvorn (see Walaker Hotel recommendation)
you can catch the fjerry across the fjord to Urnes, where a
steep but pleasant 20-minute walk takes you to Norway's
oldest stave church (1150) and the most important artistic
and historic sight in the region (mid-June through mid-
August, 10:30-17:30). Ferries leave Solvorn between 10:00
and 16:30 (ten-minute ride, 28 kr round-trip; if the car
ferry is running and you're skipping the glacier, you may
want to drive down the Urnes side of the fjord and cross
to Solvorn).

▲▲**Jostedalsbre**—Your best chance for a hands-on glacier experience is to visit the Jostedalsbre's Nigardsbreen
"tongue." This most accessible branch of mainland
Europe's largest glacier (185 square miles) is an easy drive
up Jostedal from Lusterfjorden. From Gaupne, drive up
road #604 for 23 miles to Elvekrok where you take the
private toll road (15 kr) for 2½ miles to the lake. (Look for
Breheimsentereth, a new information center on the glacier and its history at the entrance to the Nigard Glacier
valley, new in 1991, tel. 056/83275.) From here take the
special boat (10:00-18:00, mid-June through mid-August,
10 kr round-trip) to within 30 minutes' walk of the glacier
itself. The walk is steep and slippery in places. Follow the

red marks. There are 90-minute guided "family" walks of the glacier (daily at 12:00 and 14:00, minimum age is five, I'd rate them PG-13 myself) for 50 kr. Tougher glacier hikes (4 hours, 190 kr, equipment rentable there) also go daily. The glacier is a powerful river of ice, and nearly every year tourists are killed by it. The guided walk is safest and exciting enough. Use the Gaupne TI (tel. 056/81211, or 83273) to confirm your plans and the rather complicated timing (three hours from Boverdal to the car park, 15 minutes on the boat, 30-minute hike, picnic break, if you leave at 9:00, you can make the 14:00 tour). If this is your first glacier, it's worth the time and hike even without the tour. If glaciers don't give you tingles and you're feeling pressed, skip it.

Sogn Folkemuseum—Between Sogndal and Kaupanger is this fine look at the region's folk culture. English tours are available—sometimes on request. (20 kr, mid-May through September, 10:00-19:00, tel. 78206.) This is a great place to kill time if you're waiting for the Kaupanger-Revsnes ferry. The little stave-type church at the edge of Kaupanger is worth a free peek.

Kaupanger—Revsnes—Hornadalen—Aurland
Today's finale takes us over another incredible mountain pass, gives us the classic fjord aerial view, and winds us into the pleasant fjord-side town of Aurland. Catch the Kaupanger-Revsnes ferry (15 minutes; at least hourly departures including 15:00, 15:45, 17:00, 17:50, and 19:00; 40 kr for car, driver, and passenger; call 056/78116 on summer weekends for a free reservation). Leave E-68 at Erdal to make the wildly scenic and treacherous 90-minute drive to Aurland over 4,000-foot-high Hornadalen. This summer-only road is the most scenic I've experienced. You'll pass remote mountain huts, terrifying mountain views, and survive a twelve-hairpin zigzag descent into the Aurland fjord with the best fjord views this lifetime has to offer. Stop at the first fjord view point as you begin your descent, it's the best. This is a tough day. There's simply not enough time to do it and the gla-

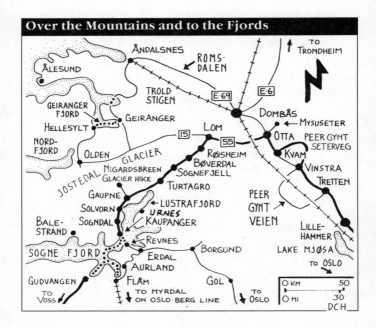

Over the Mountains and to the Fjords

cier walk comfortably. You could add another day and do this tomorrow morning. Be careful! A surprise summer snowstorm on Hornadalen Pass nearly made this, the first of my books, a posthumous publication.

Accommodations on Sognefjord

Sogndal, about a ten-minute drive from the Kaupanger ferry, is the only sizable town before you cross Sognefjord. It's big enough to have a helpful TI (tel. 056/71161, can find cheap rooms in private homes) and a busy shopping street. For budget rooms in town, try the home of **Bjarne and Ella Skieldestad** (110 kr per person, 75 kr without bedding, on the town's main drag at Gravensteinsgate 10, tel. 056/72183), the home of **Ingleiv Kram** (tel. 71383), the **Loftenes** pensjonat (380 kr per double with breakfast, near the water, tel. 056/71577), or the **youth hostel** (beds in 1-, 2-, or 3-bed rooms for 70 kr to 100 kr, hot meals and members' kitchen, at the fork in the road as you enter town, tel. 056/72033, closed 10:30-16:30).

Walaker Hotel—For 300 years (tricentennial in 1990), the Walaker family has run this former inn and coach station. In the main house, tradition drips like butter through the halls and living rooms. The rooms are simple but good, and a warm family feeling pervades. The modern annex is basic and functional. The Walaker, set right on the Lusterfjord, in the perfect garden to get over a mental breakdown, is open May through September. Oda and Hermod Walaker serve fine food and are a wealth of information and help. Doubles range from 450 to 700 kr including breakfast. A little less painful to budget travelers might be their 4-bed flats that rent for 380 kr without sheets. This is the only hotel in Solvorn, a sleepy little Victorian town, a two-mile deadend off route 55, ten miles east of Sogndal. The town's tiny boat or ferry crosses the fjord regularly to Urnes and Norway's oldest stave church (see above).

Kaupanger—This town is a ferry landing set on the scenic Sognefjord, and little more. To spend the night, consider one of two "husroms" (room in a private home-type option). Both are funky, right on the water beyond the dock, with seagulls and a view. The **Ylvisaker** family (4-person loft in a boat house, key in main house above, often booked up, tel. 056/78360) and **Mrs. Lund** (farther down the coast in a house with a porch you could fish from, she speaks no English, tel. 056/78366) each charge about 100 kr per person for their simple double rooms.

Accommodations in Aurland
Aabelheim Pension—Located right in the town center, friendly old Gurid Stigen runs far and away Aurland's best "cozy like a farmhouse" place. Gurid speaks only Norwegian, but she laughs in any language. (Cozy is *koselig*, a good Norwegian word.) You'll pay 280 kr for one of six doubles and a very traditional award-winning living room. (Open mid-June to mid-September, breakfast 50 kr extra, tel. 056/33449.)

Vangen Motel—Also nestled in downtown Aurland, this simple old hotel offers very basic rooms (all with pri-

vate showers). Doubles are 300 kr, or only 200 if you provide the sheets. There's a big self-serve kitchen, dining,
and living area. Open all year. The motel has four-bed
huts right on the beach for 200 kr without sheets, tel.
056/33580.

Aurland Fjord Hotel—This is a modern place with
more comfort and less traditional coziness. Basic restaurant, central location, friendly, the only pub in town.
Doubles cost 600 kr with breakfast, including shower.
Tel. 056/33505.

Accommodations in Flam
Heimly Lodge—This place is doing its best to go big-
time in a small-time town. It's clean and efficient and is
the best normal hotel in town. 550 kr doubles with
breakfast and shower. Sit on the porch with new friends
and watch the clouds roll down the fjord. Located 400
yards along the harbor from the station. Tel. 056/32241.

Youth Hostel—Run by the Heimly Lodge people, the
youth hostel is just behind the Heimly Lodge. 70 kr per
bed in a double, 6 kr for a shower. Tel. 056/32241.

Flam Camping—The cheapest beds in the area are on
the river just behind the Flam train station where the
Holand family runs a campground with dorm beds in
4-bed bungalows (60 kr per bed with kichenette, 15 kr
for sheets). They also have 200 kr doubles with bedding,
4-bed cabins for 225 kr, and a deluxe cabin for 450 kr.
Tel. 056/32121.

SOGNEFJORD CRUISE, "NORWAY IN A NUTSHELL," AND INTO BERGEN

While Norway has great mountains, her greatest claim to scenic fame is her deep and lush fjords. A series of well-organized and spectacular bus, train, and ferry connections, appropriately called "Norway in a Nutshell," lays Norway's most beautiful fjord country spread eagle on a scenic platter. This is the seductive Sognefjord—tiny but tough ferries, towering narrow canyons, isolated farms and villages steeped in the mist of countless waterfalls. You're an eager Lilliputian on the Norwegian Gulliver of nature. The day ends with the road, in Bergen.

Suggested Schedule

9:10	Catch the ferry from Aurland to Gudvangen for the very best of fjord country, "Norway in a Nutshell."
11:00	Arrive in Gudvangen, coffee and a good strong view at the Stalheim hotel.
12:30	Picnic at Tvindefossen waterfall.
13:30	Drive the 75 miles from Voss to Bergen on lucky route #13.
16:00	Arrive Bergen. Possible visit to Grieg's home, Stave Church before checking into room.
19:00	Trip up the Floybanen (funicular) to Floyen for a city view and dinner. Drop by the tourist office to plan for tomorrow.

Transportation

Car ferries and express boats connect towns along the Sognefjord and Bergen. Ferries go where you need them and cost roughly $4 per hour for walk-ons and $14 per hour for a car, driver, and passenger. Reservations are generally not necessary and sometimes not possible, but in summer, especially on Fridays and Sundays, I'd get one to be safe (tel. 056/78116, free and easy).

Public Transportation Around Sognefjord

Car Ferries

From . . .To	Length of Trip	Trips in Each Direction Daily
Kaupanger-Revsnes	15 minutes	20 a day
Revsnes-Gudvangen	2 hours	2-5 a day
Kaupanger-Gudvangen	2 hours	2-5 a day
Kaupanger-Aurland-Flam	2½ hours	1 a day
Aurland-Gudvangen	1½ hours	2-3 a day
Flam-Gudvangen	2 hours	1-2 a day

Coastal Express Boat (expensive)

Bergen-Flam	5 hours	1-2 a day
Bergen-Stavanger	5 hours	2 a day

Buses

Voss-Sogndal	3 hours	3 a day in summer
Otta-Lom-Sogndal	5 hours	2 a day in summer
Revnes-Aurland over Hornadalen	2¼ hours	1 a day

For reservations: ferries—056/78116, buses and express boats—05/324015

Sightseeing Highlights—"Norway in a Nutshell"

▲▲▲ **Sognefjord—Aurlandsfjord**—Everything up to now has been merely foreplay. This is it—the ultimate natural thrill Norway has to offer. The entire west coast is slashed by stunning fjords, but the Sognefjord, Norway's longest (120 miles) and deepest (over a mile), is tops. Aurlandsfjord, a remote, scenic, and accessible arm of the Sognefjord, is possibly the juiciest bite in the scenic pomegranate of Norway. The local weather is actually decent, with about 24 inches of rain per year compared to over 6 feet annually in nearby Bergen.

▲ **Flam**, at the head of the Aurlandsfjord, is on the "Norway in a Nutshell" route. Very scenic and fairly touristed, it's little more than a train station, ferry landing, and cluster of hotels and hostels. (TI tel. 056/32106, open daily, May-September 8:15-20:30.)

▲▲ **Aurland**, a few miles down the coast, is more of a

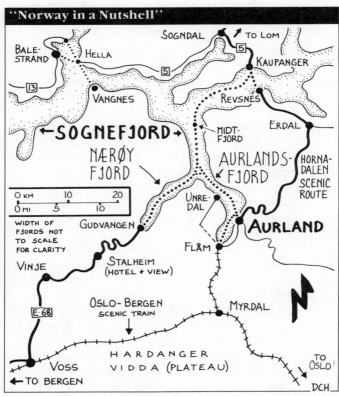

"Norway in a Nutshell"

BALE-STRAND — HELLA — SOGNDAL — TO LOM — KAUPANGER — VANGNES — REVSNES — ERDAL — SOGNEFJORD — NÆRØY FJORD — MIDT-FJORD — AURLANDS-FJORD — HORNA-DALEN SCENIC ROUTE — UNRE-DAL — AURLAND — GUDVANGEN — FLÅM — VINJE — STALHEIM (HOTEL & VIEW) — OSLO-BERGEN SCENIC TRAIN — MYRDAL — E·68 — VOSS — ← TO BERGEN — HARDANGER VIDDA (PLATEAU) — TO OSLO

0 KM 10 20
0 MI 5 10
WIDTH OF FJORDS NOT TO SCALE FOR CLARITY

DCH

town and less of a tourist depot. Nothing exciting, but it's a good easygoing fjord-side home base. You can hike up the valley, or tour the electrical works (public tours show visitors the source of most of Oslo's electricity daily from mid-June to mid-August, Monday-Saturday at 13:00, Sunday at 16:00, tel. 33292). The harborside public library is a pleasant refuge, and the 800-year-old church is worth a look. The area has as many goats as people (1,800). The one who runs the tourist office (mid-June through August, daily, 11:00-19:00, pick up the English-language Bergen guide) speaks English and can be phoned at 056/33313 or 33323. The local geitost (goat's cheese) is sweet and delicious. (Note: every train arriving in Flam connects with a bus to Aurland. Nine buses and four fer-

ries connect the towns daily.) Nearest bike rental is at the
Flam TI.

▲**Unredal** is an almost impossibly remote community
of 52 families that, until the road from Flam was opened
in 1985, was reached only by boat. It has Norway's
smallest still-used church (twelfth century). If you're
looking for remoteness, this is it. The 15-minute drive
from Flam includes a strange no-lines-no-lights up-hill-
all-the-way tunnel experience. There's not much in the
town, so famous for its goat's cheese and small church,
but I'll never forget the picnic I had on the ferry wharf. If
you want the ferry to stop, turn on the blinking light.
You'll sail by Unredal on your boat trip to Gudvangen.

In 1992 they plan to open the tunnel to Gudvangen
(fifth longest in the world), which will bring more than
goats to little Unredal.

▲▲▲**Flam-Aurland (or Kaupanger)-Gudvangen
fjord cruise**—The post boat takes more tourists than
mail on this breathtaking voyage. For 90 minutes camera-
clicking tourists scurry on the drool-stained deck like
nervous roosters scratching fitfully for the photo to catch
the magic. The boat stops at whichever isolated farm has
mail. Sometimes two ferries hook up at the junction of
two fjords to let passengers and mail change over. Waterfalls turn the black rock cliffs into a bridal fair and you
can nearly reach out and touch the sheer cliffs of the awe-
some Naeroyfjord. The ride is the ultimate fjord experience (Geiranger doesn't begin to compare). It's one of
those fine times, like when you're high on the tip of an
Alp, when a warm camaraderie spontaneously combusts
between all the strangers who came together for the
experience.

You'll get plenty of glorious scenery, whether you start
from Kaupanger (2-hour trips depart daily at 8:50, 11:40,
and 14:45) or Aurland (90-minute trips daily, 9:10 and
15:00 departures, about 100 kr for car and driver, 30 kr
for passenger or walk-on, call 056/78116 for reservations
if you have a car). The ferry starts in Flam a few minutes
before Aurland, but cars must board at Aurland. The sce-

nic express boat to Bergen leaves Flam daily in June, July, and August at 15:00, stopping in Aurland and covering most of the Sognefjord before it arrives in Bergen at 21:30 (about 400 kr or 200 with a train pass or hotel card, per person). While the Aurland fjord is great and the Kaupanger boat misses that, both boats do the Naeroy-fjord, which is the most staggering.

From Gudvangen to Bergen
Gudvangen-Stalheim-Voss-Bergen: From the boat dock in Gudvangen, you'll continue by car or bus up the Naeroydalen ("Narrow Valley") past a river bubbling excitedly about the plunge it just took. You'll see the two giant falls just before the road marked "Stalheimskleiva." Stop to see the falls before taking the Stalheimskleiva road. This incredible road worms its way doggedly up into the ozone. I overheated my car in a few minutes. Take it, but take it easy. (The main road gets you there easier—through a tunnel and 1.3 km back up a smaller road.) At the top, stop for coffee at the friendly but very, very touristy Stalheim Hotel. This huge eagle's nest hotel is a stop for just about every tour group that ever saw a fjord. Genuine trolls sew the pewter buttons on the sweaters here, but a cup of coffee is only 8 kr and the priceless view is free.

The road continues into a mellower beauty past lakes and farms toward Voss. Stop at the Tvindefossen, a water-fall with a handy campground/WC/kiosk picnic area right under it. Unless you judge waterfalls by megaton-nage, this 150-yard-long fall has nuclear charms. The grassy plateau and flat rocks at its base were made espe-cially for your picnic lunch.

At Voss the road to Bergen forks. The big road (E68-Bergen) is the more congested, but less treacherous, major route into Bergen. But since we're still high on Nor-wegian scenery, let's take the small, windy one, lucky 13 (75 miles, 2 ½ hours to Bergen). The barren but scenic road to Dale is very narrow with sparse traffic (all the heavy traffic takes E-68), lots of summer cabins, nothing

much more. Take a rest ogle at the dam (after Brekke).
From the parking place there, you can look down at the
pigtail switchbacks into Dale and marvel at my knack for
finding exciting roads. After Dale, it's light traffic and dark
tunnels into Bergen. The road gets better and the landscape stays fjordic.

At the edge of Bergen (on E-68) you'll see signs for
Troldhaugen. If you're visiting Edvard Grieg's home and
the nearby Fantoft stave church, now is the ideal time
since you'll be driving right by them. Both are overrated
but kind of obligatory, a headache from downtown and
open until 17:30.

▲▲**The Oslo-Bergen Train**— This is simply the most
spectacular train ride in northern Europe. You'll hang out
the window with your camera smoking as you roar over
Norway's mountainous spine. The barren, windswept
heaths, glaciers, deep forests, countless lakes, and a few
rugged ski resorts create a harsh beauty. The line, an
amazing engineering feat completed in 1909, is 300 miles
long, peaks at 4,266 feet, which—at this Alaskan
latitude—is far above the tree line, goes under 18 miles of
snow sheds, over 300 bridges, and through 200 tunnels
in just under 7 hours. (450 kr, departures at about 7:30,
10:00, 15:00, and 22:30 daily in both directions, reservations required.)

▲▲**Myrdal-Flam Train**— This little 12-mile spur line
leaves the Oslo-Bergen line at Myrdal (2,800 feet) and
winds down to Flam (sea level) in 50 thrilling minutes. It's
party time on board as everyone there is doing the same
thing—living well. The conductor even stops the train
for photos at the best waterfall. This line has 20 tunnels
(over three miles' worth) and is so steep that the train has
five separate braking systems. Hikers can get off at Berek-
vam or Dalsbotn and enjoy the last half of the trip alone
on foot (two hours). This train ride is so spectacular that
drivers with the time to spare may want to do it round-
trip from Flam. Myrdal is nothing but a scenic train
junction.

▲▲▲**"Norway in a Nutshell"**— The most exciting single day trip you could make from Oslo or Bergen is this circular train-boat/bus-train trip through the chunk of fjord country I've been raving about. Rushed travelers zip in and out by train from the big cities. Those with more time do the "nutshell" segments at their leisure. It's famous, everybody does it, and, I'm afraid, if you're looking for the scenic grandeur of Norway, so should you.

The all-day trip goes by train every morning from Oslo and Bergen. Tourist offices have brochures with exact times. It's a handy round-trip or an exciting way to connect the two cities. The trip includes (as described above) the Oslo-Bergen train, the spur Myrdal-Flam train, the Flam-Gudvangen cruise, and the Gudvangen-Voss bus trip (on E-68). From Oslo, if you have only a day, I'd do Norway in a Nutshell to Bergen, enjoy the evening there, and catch the night train back.

Voss is an ugly town in a lovely lake and mountain setting. It does have an interesting folk museum, a thirteenth-century church and a few other historic sights, but it's basically a home base for summer or winter sports. The tourist office (tel. 05/511716, open 9:00-19:00, shorter Sundays and off-season) can find you a room but I'd drive right through or stay in its luxurious youth hostel. They say "Vossing Town" is the ancestral home of our first president . . . and Knute Rockne.

Accommodations in Voss: Voss hotels are modern and expensive. Its pensions are modern and a bit less expensive. If you simply refuse to hostel, the **Vang Pensjonat** (tel. 512145) and the **Kringsja Pension** (tel. 511627) offer good doubles for 480 kr including a large traditional breakfast. Both are very central. **The Voss Youth Hostel** (IYHF) is a modern (automatic sliding doors and electric eye toilet flushers), luxurious, lakeside, all-are-welcome place that almost redefines hosteling. Just a ten-minute walk on the Bergen Road from the station, the charges are 80 kr per bed (40 kr for breakfast, family rooms with two or four beds rent for 300 kr). Voss YH, Postboks 305, 5701 Voss, tel. 05/512017.

The "Golden Route" Option

This takes two extra days and a swing farther north. To cover the west of Norway more thoroughly, seeing more wild fjord and mountain beauty plus the interesting city of Alesund, consider this two-day extension to the north.

Leave our 22 Day plan near Lom and continue up the Gudbrandsdalen Valley. At Dombas, follow Romsdalen past the 3,000-foot sheer rock face of the "Troll's Wall" to Andalsnes, where you'll either detour to the "art nouveau" town of Alesund or climb south over the famous switchback Trollstigveien mountain pass.

You'll cruise the very popular and impressive Geiranger Fjord and either rejoin the basic tour at Lom or continue south to the Jostedals Glacier and along more fjords to the prestigious resort of Balestrand. From here, you'll cruise the Sognefjord to Gudvangen and on into Bergen.

Bergen

Bergen, Norway's most historic city, is permanently salted with robust cobbles and a rich sea-trading heritage. Norway's capital in the twelfth and thirteenth centuries, its wealth and importance were due to its membership in the heavyweight medieval trading club of merchant cities called the Hanseatic League. It's a romantic place with a colorful harborside fish market, old atmospheric "Hanseatic" quarter, and great people watching. Famous for its lousy weather, Bergen gets an average of 80 inches of rain annually (compared to 30 in Oslo). Sixty days of sunshine is a good year. With 210,000 people, it has its big city tension, parking problems, and high prices. But visitors stick mainly to the old center—easily handled on foot—and, with the help of the friendly tourist office, you'll manage just fine. Bergen is seven scenic hours (240 miles) from Oslo by train. Any visit to Norway needs a stop here.

Tourist Office: Right downtown, this energetic office will handle all your Bergen and West Norway information needs. For a 15 kr fee (20 kr for two) they'll set you up in a private room or hotel. Pick up any sightseeing brochures you need, confirm your sightseeing plans and ask about

town and fjord tours. They change money at 4 percent
less than the banks (but with no 10 to 20 kr per check fee
for traveler's checks, so they're great for small exchanges
or the poor souls who didn't read this book's introduction and brought $20 checks to Norway). They also have
information and tickets for tours and concerts and a daily
events board. At Torgalmenning, a bright and busy kiosk
on the pedestrian square just off the harbor, five minutes
walk from the train station, tel. 05/321480. Open May-
September, Monday through Saturday 8:30-21:00, Sunday 10:00-19:00, off-season Monday-Saturday
10:00-15:00. The free "Bergen Guide" lists all sights,
hours, and special events and has a fine map. Buses cost
11 kr per ride or 45 kr for a 48-hour "Tourist Ticket."

Need to reconfirm your flight? Do it three days in
advance. (SAS in Bergen is at 05/236330.)

Accommodations in Bergen

July through mid-August is peak season for rainy Bergen,
but you should find a room just about any time without a
reservation. The hotel scene is bleak (minimum 550 kr
doubles with breakfast), with none of the great summer
discounts found in other big Nordic cities. But if you can
handle showers down the hall and cook breakfast yourself in the communal kitchens, several pensions offer better rooms with a homey atmosphere and a fine central
location for half the hotel prices. The private homes I list
are cheap, central, and quite professional. The cheapest
dorm/hostel-style beds are not much less then the private homes and unless the shoestring you're traveling on
is really frazzled or you like to hang out with other vaga-
bonds and hostelers, I'd stick with the private rooms.
Keep in mind that the tourist office is very helpful in finding the least expensive rooms, but if you call direct you'll
save yourself the TI fee (15-20 kr) and save your hostess
10 percent.

If you must have a uniformed person behind the key
desk, the prestigious old **Hotel Hordaheimen** is very
central, just off the harbor, and your best budget hotel

bet. Run by the same alcohol-free, give-the-working-man-a-break organization that brought you the Kaffistova restaurants, their prices are 480 to 700 kr for doubles with a fine breakfast. If you want the cheapest room, you must ask for it. Their cafeteria, open late, serves traditional, basic (drab) inexpensive meals. 18 C. Sundts Gate, tel. 05/232320.

Mycklebust Pension is a family-run place that is an explosion of homeyness, offering better rooms than the Hordaheimen but pension rather than hotel services. It's friendly, central (a 5-minute walk to market), with your own kitchen and laundry service, and showers down the hall. (Doubles from 350-380 kr, or 600 kr for four people in a great family room. 19 Rosenberggate, tel. 901670.)

Globex Inn Pensjonat is newly opened, modern, bright, clean, and very comfortable. It is centrally located and has a great communal kitchen but is rather sterile (300 kr doubles, 400 kr family-of-four rooms, showers down the hall, no breakfast, 3 blocks from the TI at Jon Smorsgata 11, N-5011 Bergan, tel. 05/231860).

Kloster Pension in a funky cobbled neighborhood four blocks off the harbor has basic 330 kr doubles including breakfast. 12 Klosteret, tel. 318666. **Fagerheim Pension**, open only mid-May to mid-September, offers some of the cheapest doubles in town (250-300 kr, breakfast extra; 49 Kalvedalsveien, up King Oscar's Gate half a mile, tel. 310172). **Park Pension** is very classy, nearly a hotel, in a wonderful neighborhood—central but residential. People who have the money for a cheap hotel but want classy Old World lived-in elegance love this place (500-600 kr for doubles with breakfast, 35 Harold Harfagres Gate, tel. 230486).

Private homes: The TI sets people up in local homes for 220 to 260 kr per double. These are normally friendly, comfortable, and central or with easy bus access. In summer they are often all taken by noon. Since the Bergen hotels don't quite understand the magic of the marketplace, there are more private homes than ever opening up. Here are three you can book direct (to save you the booking fee and your hosts the TI commission): **Alf and Elizabeth Heskja** are a young couple with four good double rooms, a kitchen, and facilities down the hall. Located just 3 minutes from the train station on a steep cobbled lane (ground floor) near the harbor. This is far better than the hostel for budget train travelers. Call in advance. 17 Skivebakken, tel. 315955. On the same street is the **Olsnes home**, with 5 very comfortable doubles and 3 singles, 24 Skivebakken, tel. 312044. These are both very cheap and central and are quite private, lacking a lot of chatty interaction with your hosts. The **Vagenes** family has four doubles in a large comfortable house on the edge of town. Not so central, but 10 minutes from downtown on bus #19. From downtown cross the Pud-defjordsbroen bridge (road 555), go through the tunnel, turn left on J.L. Mowinckelsvei until you reach Helgeplasset Street just past the "Hogesenter" (only 200 kr per double, J.L. Mowinckelsvei 95, tel. 05/161101).

Youth and Hostel Beds
Intermission—Open mid-June through mid-August, 8:00-11:00 and 17:00-23:00 only, offers 20 cheap mattresses on one coed floor for 75 kr. Lockers, kitchen, washing machine, and rental bikes are available (Kalfarsveien 8, a 5-minute walk from the train station, tel. 05/313275).

   Interpoint/YMCA—Even cheaper. For 65 kr, you get a mattress on the floor in 30-person rooms, one for boys and one for others. Open 8:00-11:00, 17:00-24:00, summer only. Ten minutes from the station, Kalfarveien 77, tel. 05/320746.

   Montana Youth Hostel (IYHF)—One of Europe's best hostels, its drawbacks are its remote location and relatively high price. Still, the bus connections (#4, 20 minutes from the center) and the facilities (modern 5-bed rooms, classy living room, no curfew, huge parking lot) are excellent. 90 kr per bed, family rooms for couples with children. The breakfast is not worthwhile, and there's no members' kitchen (plan a picnic in the lounge,

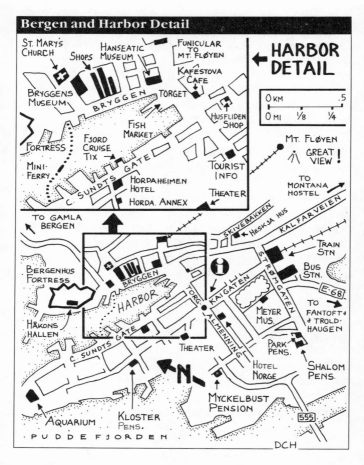

Bergen and Harbor Detail

← HARBOR DETAIL

instead), but it's very well run and friendly. 30 Johan Blydts Vei, tel. 292900.

Food

As in Oslo the **Kaffistova Cafeteria**, facing the fish market, is a good basic food value. Fine atmosphere (ground floor—better than fast food; 1st floor—self-service cafeteria; 2nd floor—cafe serving meals), ground floor open until 22:00 (good hot pancake meat rolls), cafe only until 19:00, closed earlier off-season. For more traditional Norwegian fare, eat at the **Hordaheimen Hotel's cafeteria**—great prices and lots of lefse, but a bit dreary.

Bryggeloffet and Bryggestuen, one restaurant on two levels with two different styles at #6 in the Bryggen harborfront, offers great (but smokey) atmosphere, good value for Norway, and good seafood meals for around 100 kr. Small servings but more potatoes on request. Dagens Menu—60 kr (off-season only). There are plenty of classy atmospheric places along the Bryggen harborfront; several are surprisingly affordable. The **Unicorn** offers Bergen's top seafood buffet but is quite expensive (140 kr, Monday-Saturday 12:00-16:00).

Hotel Norge's "Kaltbord" buffet—Bergen's ritziest hotel is famous for its daily (11:30-17:00) all-you-can-eat spread served in its classy Ole Bull restaurant—hot dishes, seafood, desserts rich in memories and calories. 145 kr. Their 60 kr breakfast is also a worthy splurge. Just past the tourist office.

The **Augusta Conditori and Lunchsalon** (next to Hotel Hordaheimen) serves good meals at a reasonable price in cheery-classy atmosphere. Open 10:00-18:00, at C. Sundtsgate 24.

Bergen's "in" cafes are stylish, cozy, small, open very late, and a great place to experience the local Yuppie scene. The **Cafe Opera** (50 kr dinners, 30 kr soup and bread specials, often with live music, always with live locals, English newspapers, chess, open till wee hours) and **Cafe Henrik** are on Vasker Elven near the theater.

The **Zachariassbryggen** is a good pub and wine bar with piano music (open late, popular with locals) located right on the Torget, or harbor square.

For a louder crowd and a younger scene, you can eat well and drink cheap at the **Maxime Bergen's Polar Bear Bar** (light lunches for 30 kr, "cheapest dinners in town," Ole Bulls Plass 9, around the corner from the taxi station and TI, food until about 20:00).

BERGEN

Bergen has a rugged charm. Norway's capital long before Oslo, she wears her rich Hanseatic heritage proudly. The town seems made for a tourist, with a colorful market, a small easy-on-foot old quarter, and a little mountain right downtown that comes complete with a handy lift to zip visitors up for the view. With this busy Bergen day, you will have seen the five major cities of Scandinavia.

Suggested Schedule

9:00	Shop, explore the center around the tourist office (open 8:30, check plans).
10:00	Fish market and Hanseatic Quarter.
11:00	Walking tour of old town from Bryggens Museum.
12:30	Picnic.
14:30	Shop, spend more time in Hanseatic Quarter (your tour ticket is good for the museums all day), go out to Gamle Bergen, take the hourly Hakon Hall tour, little train, or harbor tour, or really pig out at Hotel Norge's classy buffet dinner (closes at 17:00).

Sightseeing Highlights

▲▲▲ **Hanseatic Quarter**—Called the "German Wharf" until 1940, now just called the wharf or "Bryggen," this is the city's old German trading center. From 1370 to 1754, German merchants controlled Bergen's trade. In 1550, it was a German city of 2,000 workaholic merchants— walled and surrounded by 8,000 Norwegians in Bergen. Bryggen, which has burned down several times, is now gentrified and boutiquish but still lots of fun. Explore. You'll find plenty of shops, restaurants, planky alleys, leaning old wooden warehouses, good browsing, atmospheric eating, and two worthwhile museums. (The tours and museums described below are each three-star sights.)

Every day at 11:00 and 13:00 from mid-May through August, a local historian takes visitors on a 90-minute walk through the old Hanseatic town. This is a great way to get an understanding of Bergen's 900 years of history. Tours cost 40 kr and leave from the Bryggens Museum. This fee includes the 10 kr entry tickets to, and tours of, the Hanseatic and Bryggens museums and the medieval assembly rooms called the "Schotstuene" (worthwhile only with a guide, and then very). Tel. 316710.

The Hanseatic Museum is a very atmospheric old merchant house furnished with dried fish, old ropes, an old ox tail used for wringing spilled cod liver oil back into the bucket, sagging steps and cupboard beds from the early 1700s (one with a medieval pin-up). This wonderful little museum is open daily from 10:00 to 17:00, May and September 11:00 to 14:00, 10 kr (included on Bryggen tour). Drop in and ask when the next sporadic but very good English tour is scheduled (tel. 314189).

Bryggens Museum, a new modern museum on the archaeological site of the earliest Bergen (1050-1500), with interesting temporary exhibits upstairs, offers almost no English information (if you take the tour, the fine 20 kr English guide book is unnecessary). You can see the actual excavation—half the museum—for free from the window just below St. Mary's Church. Open May through August, Monday, Wednesday, Friday 10:00-16:00, Tuesday and Thursday 10:00-20:00, Saturday-Sunday 11:00-15:00; September-April, Monday through Friday 11:00-15:00, Saturday and Sunday 12:00-15:00, 10 kr, tel. 316710. There is a good inexpensive cafeteria with soup and bread specials.

St. Mary's Church is Bergen's oldest building and one of Norway's finest churches from about 1150. Open summer, Monday through Saturday, 11:00 to 16:00.

Bergen's famous fish market bustles nearby, Monday-Saturday from 10:00 to 16:00, offering lots of smelly photo fun. Don't miss it. All of these Hanseatic sights are within 2 minutes walk of each other.

▲▲**Floybanen**—Just two blocks from the fish market is

the steep funicular ride to the top of "Mount" Floyen
(1,000 feet up) for the best view in town of the town, sur-
rounding islands, and fjords all the way to the west coast.
There are endless hikes on top and a pleasant walk back
down into Bergen. It's a popular picnic or pizza-to-go
perch. (26 kr round-trip, departures each way on the half
hour and often on the quarter hour.)

▲▲**Wandering**—Bergen is a great strolling town. The
harborfront is a great place to kick back and watch the
pigeons mate. Other good areas to explore are around
Klostergate, Knosesmanet, Ytre Markevei, and the area
behind Bryggen. The modern town, around the TI, also
has a pleasant ambience. For a musical interlude, most
Norwegian record shops have a bank of earphones so
browsers can "sample" the records of their choice. The
best buses for a city joy ride are #1 and #4. A little red
ferry chugs across the harbor every half hour for 7 kr. It's
a handy shortcut with great harbor views.

▲**Aquarium**—Small but great fun if you like fish, this
aquarium, wonderfully laid out and explained in English,
claims to be the second-most-visited sight in Norway.
Pleasant ten-minute walk from the center. Cheery cafeteria
(with fresh fish sandwiches). Daily 9:00-20:00, 22 kr.

▲**Old Bergen**—"Gamle Bergen" is a Disney-cute
gathering of thirty-five eighteenth- and nineteenth-
century shops and houses offering a pleasant cobbled
look at "the old life." Open daily from mid-May to early
September from 12:00 to 18:00, mid-June through mid-
August from 11:00-19:00, with English guided tours on
the hour, 20 kr, bus #1 or #9, from the post office (direction Conborg) to Gamle Bergen (first stop after tunnel),
tel. 257034.

▲**Various City Tours**—The tourist information center
organizes two other tours—a daily 75-minute intro at
9:30 for 60 kr and a daily 2-hour intro at 11:00 for 90 kr.
They leave from Hotel Norge next to the TI. These are
barely worthwhile for a quick orientation. Info tel.
05/299543. More fun and plenty informative, if you're
into city tours, are the harbor tours (aboard the *White*

Lady, tel. 314320, from the fish market) and the tacky tourist train with English headphones tours (from the TI). Both cost a krown a minute for 50 minutes and leave on the hour.

▲**Fantoft Stave Church**—The huge preserved-in-tar, most touristy stave church in Norway is situated in a quiet forest next to a mysterious stone cross and has a beautifully decorated interior. It's difficult to really understand this twelfth-century wooden church without a tour. It's bigger but no better than others covered in this itinerary. Worth a look if you're in the neighborhood, even after hours, for its evocative setting. Open mid-May through mid-September, 10:30-13:30 and 14:30-17:30. 7 kr.

▲**Grieg's Home, Troldhaugen**—Norway's greatest composer spent his last years here (1885-1907) soaking in inspirational fjord beauty and composing many of his greatest works. In a very romantic Victorian setting, the ambience of the place is pleasant even for non-fans and essential to anyone who knows and loves Grieg's music. The house is full of memories, and his little studio hut near the water makes you want to sit down and write a song. Unfortunately, it gets the "worst presentation in Scandinavia for a historical sight" award—mobbed with tour groups, nothing in English, and no imagination in mixing Grieg's music with the house. Daily, May-September 9:30-13:30, 14:30-17:30, 10 kr. Ask the tourist office about concerts (Wednesdays and Sundays at 20:00 in June and July and other days sporadically).

Fantoft and Troldhaugen, obligations on the typical tourist checklist, are both a headache to reach without a car (the easy-to remember public transit directions—20 minutes on bus #20 from the station and a 20-minute walk—are well explained in the TI's free "Bergen Guide" pamphlet). The daily bus tour (15:30-18:30, 125 kr) is worthwhile for the very informative guide and the easy transportation. If you've seen other stave churches and can't whistle anything by Grieg, skip them. Drivers will pass both sights as they enter and leave Bergen on E-68. When you see a campground, "Tennis Paradise" center, and a Kro restaurant at the edge of town, you're close. Stop and ask for help. The stave church is just down road 14 off E-68 at the "Philips System Forhandler" shop. Troldhaugen is clearly marked off E-68.

Shopping—The Husfliden Shop just off the market at 3 Vagsalmenning is a fine place for handmade Norwegian sweaters and goodies. Good variety but not cheap. Like most shops, it's open Monday-Friday 9:00-16:30, Thursday evening until 19:00, Saturday 9:00-14:00. Major shops are closed on Sundays, but shop-till-you-drop tourists manage to find plenty of action even on the day of rest.

Folk Evenings—The "Fana Folklore" show is Bergen's most advertised folk evening. It's a very touristy collection of cultural clichés with unexciting food, music, dancing, and colorful costumes on an old farm. Many think it's too gimmicky, but many others think it's lots of fun. 150 kr includes the short bus trip and a meager dinner. Most nights from late May to early September, 19:00-22:30, tel. 915240.

The Bergen Folklore show is a smaller, less gimmicky program featuring a good music-and-dance look at rural and traditional Norway. Performances are right downtown at the Bryggens Museum every Monday and Wednesday at 20:30 from mid-June through mid-August. Tickets for the one-hour show are 50 kr at the TI or at the door. Tel. 248929 or 134506.

An Atlantic coast side trip? Dotted with villages, the nearby rugged Atlantic coast of Norway is a brisk switch from all the fjord beauty. The small windswept town of Bloomvag (with the Pension Maken, at the head of the bay, tel. 05/387105) is a fine retreat.

Boats from Bergen—The TI has several brochures on tours of the nearby Hardanger and Sogne fjords. There are plenty of choices. "Norway in a Nutshell," if you skipped the days before Bergen in this 22-day plan, can be done in a day from Bergen, explained in Day 15.

Itinerary Option

Bergen is an efficient place to end your tour. You can turn in your car and fly home from here. (Ask your travel agent about the economic feasibility of this "open jaws" option.) If you plugged in Days 20 and 21 after Copenhagen at the start of this trip, you'd miss nothing essential and save substantial time and piles of miles.

To travel directly from Bergen to Copenhagen, you can fly. Occasionally there are very cheap (500 kr) flights available only locally. Ask around, but don't count on it. Or, you can sail. The Fred Olsen Line (tel. 05/32 13 10) sails from Bergen to Hirtshals, northern Denmark (20 hours, one to three times a week, about 500 kr per passenger and 400 kr per car) but not at all from mid-June through the end of August. By the way, don't worry about missing Stavanger. I don't know what it's like to live there—but it's a dull place to visit.

The Norway Line sails from Bergen to Newcastle, England, two times weekly from April through December (22 hours, about $100). Summer and Friday, Saturday, and Sunday departures are most expensive; cars cost 300 kr or are free with four paying passengers. The cheapest tickets get you a "sleeperette" to stretch out on overnight. They also offer reasonable and regular crossings from Bergen to Esbjerg (Jutland, Denmark). Tel. 322780 in Bergen, or 091/2961313 in Newcastle.

SOUTH TO SETESDAL VALLEY

Today is a long drive as we round the corner and begin our return to Copenhagen. There are several scenic options. You can do the faster Hardanger Fjord route or you can island hop south from Bergen, getting a feel for Norway's rugged Atlantic coast before heading inland along a frightfully narrow fjord. Either way, you'll end up crossing a mountain pass into the remote—and therefore very traditional—Setesdal Valley.

Suggested Schedule

9:00	Drive south, slithering along another fjord or island-hopping, then inland to Setesdal.
18:00	Set up in Hovden, at the top of Setesdal.

Transportation: Driving from Bergen to Setesdal

There are two options. For speed and maximum fjord beauty (and traffic), drive E-68 from Bergen to Kvanndal, then ferry to Utne and drive #550 along the Sorfjorden to Odda. Head east on E-76 to Haukeligrend, the Gateway to Setesdal.

This route will give you a look at the famous but over-rated Hardanger Fjord. If you took route 13 into Bergen, you'll minimize backtracking (and learn why I prefer the narrower #13). With traffic, tiny fjord-hanging E-68, which is the major road connecting Oslo and Bergen, is a lunch line in Hell. I left Bergen at 6:45, followed signs E-68/Voss, had almost no traffic, and drove right on to the 9:15 ferry in Kvanndal. Save time and money by ferrying only to Utne (50 kr for car and driver, 15-minute ride, no reservations possible—another reason to leave early).

Odda: At the end of the fjord you'll hit the industrial town of Odda (well-stocked TI for whole region and beyond, tel. 054/41 297). Odda brags that Kaiser Wilhelm came here a lot, but he's dead and I'd drive right through. If you want to visit the tongue of a glacier, drive to Buer and hike an hour to Buerbreen. From Odda drive into the land of boulders, where rocks so big that trees grow on them seem to be hurled into the fields by the mighty waterfalls that almost line the road. Stop at the giant double fall (on the left, pull out on the right, drive slowly through it if you need a car wash).

Roldal: Higher up, the old town of Roldal is trying to develop some tourism. Drive straight through. Its old church isn't worth the time or money to see. You'll have no choice but to pay 30 kr for the toll road across the region's snowy rooftop. Lakes, like frosted mirrors, make desolate huts come in pairs. **Haukeliseter**, a group of sod-roofed buildings filled with cultural clichés and tour groups, offers reasonable (40-50 kr) hot meals with a great lakeside setting. If you have yet to try the traditional "romegrot" porridge, this might be a good time.

At Haukeligrend, you'll take a right and roll into Setesdal. It's all downhill from here to Denmark.

The Atlantic Coast Island-hopping Option: Interesting, relaxing, time consuming, and expensive—but I think worthwhile—is the island-hopping route down the south coast. Instead of fjords you'll see stony rugged islands and glimpses of the open sea. Leave Bergen on E-68, past the stave church and Grieg's home (you could see these on your way south, but, unfortunately they don't open til 10:30), follow route 14 to Osoyro and Halhjem, where you'll catch the ferry to Sandvikvag (60 minutes, 100 kr for car, driver and co-pilot). If you drive the speed limit for 20 miles across the island of Stord, staying on route 14, you'll catch the connecting ferry from Skersholmane to Utbjoa. It takes 35 minutes, 76 kr for car and two bodies. From Skersholmane you'll see a small town that assembles the huge North Sea oil rigs.

From Utbjoa, drive to E-76. Follow the cliff-hanging road along the Akrafjord and up into the mountains where you'll meet the route explained above just after Odda.

In Bergen, the TI has a pamphlet called "Kyst Vegen" which gives you all the ferry connections and a handy chart. Normally the Halhjem ferries leave on the hour all day and the Skersholmane ferry leaves for Utbjoa every

90 minutes (possibly 9:30, 11:00, 12:30, 14:00, 15:30, 17:00, 18:30, and 20:00). Reservations (except maybe summer Fridays) aren't necessary.

Setesdal Valley
Hovden: Hovden is a full day's drive from Bergen, putting you right at the top of the Setesdal Valley and ready for a full and fascinating day of sightseeing as you work your way south to the coast tomorrow. Hovden is a ski resort (2,500 feet high), barren in the summer and painfully in need of charm. But it has food and beds, and it's just the right place to end today and start tomorrow.

Hovden is for nature lovers. Locals come here for a week to walk and relax. There are good walks offering a chance to see reindeer, moose, arctic fox, and rabbits— so they say. Every other day a chair lift takes summer visitors to its nearby 3,700-foot peak. The Hegni center on the lake at the south edge of town rents canoes for 15 kr an hour. In 1991 a new super indoor spa/pool complex, the Hovden Badeland, will open. This will provide a much-needed way to spend an otherwise dreary and very likely drizzly evening here. The TI is open Monday through Friday 8:00 to 16:00 all year (tel. 043/39630).

Accommodations
In Haukeligrend: Haukeli Turistheim Pensjonat offers quaint old rooms (in the quaint old half of the building), a feel-at-home Old World living room, a Ping-Pong table, no breakfast but a reasonable cafeteria, and almost never fills up in the summer (225 kr per double, at the junction of roads 76 and 12 in Haukeligrend, about 8 hours out of Bergen, 30 minutes before Hovden, tel. 036/70126).

In Hovden: Hovdehytta, a big old ski chalet with an inviting ski lodge atmosphere (large dining room, open fire in the living room), offers clean modern bunk bed doubles with a large breakfast for 330 kr. Their "anneks" has doubles with beds without sheets or breakfast for 80 kr each. Good 100 kr dinners are served. In the summer, since the place is nearly empty, there's a good chance you'll get the double to yourself. Tel. 043/39522. Built in

1911, this is the oldest place in town and the only cozy accommodations in this booming winter resort of sprawling ski ranch-style hotels.

In Valle: The **Bergtun Hotel**, an hour's drive (36 miles) south of Hovden, run by Gunnar Oiestad, is the first real cozy, old-time lodging you'll see in Setesdal. It's full of traditional furniture, paintings, and carvings in each charming room. A double with breakfast costs 380 (bunks) to 460 kr (four-poster beds). Hearty lunch specials (Dagens Ratt) with very mean Norwegian dumplings for 60 kr from 12:00 to 21:00. Valle i Setesdal, tel. 043/37270.

Itinerary Option

After what you've seen, Setesdal is less than thrilling. To save a day, you can push on to the boat to Denmark. You can call the Fred Olsen Line in Kristiansand (tel. 042/70501) and make a reservation for the midnight boat (see below for more information), have dinner at the Bergtun Hotel in Valle, and drive to the coast. Driving from Bergen to Kristiansand is a brutal but possible day. (Kristiansand is about 2½ hours from Valle; you'll need to check in at the dock by 23:00.)

SETESDAL AND ON TO DENMARK

After all the miles we covered yesterday, today is easy, with plenty of time for this cultural Easter egg hunt called Setesdal. Probably Norway's most traditional cranny, it joined the twentieth century only with the construction of the valley highway in the 1950s. This valley is a mellow montage of derelict farmhouses, sod-roofed water mills, goldsmiths and silversmiths in action, ancient churches, yellowed recipes, rivers, forests, and mountains.

Suggested Schedule

9:00	Depart Hovden.
10:00	Tour old farmstead of Bykle.
13:00	Lunch and browsing in Valle, see silver-smiths in action.
14:00	Possible fiddle show, explore your way to the coast.
18:00	Evening and dinner in port of Kris-tiansand.
22:00	Sail to Jutland, Denmark.

Sightseeing Setesdal

The most interesting route from Bergen to Norway's south coast is down Setesdal Valley ("dal" means valley, but I'll be redundant just to be doubly clear for sure). One of Norway's most traditional, undeveloped, and scenic valleys, Setesdal follows the Otra River for 140 miles south to the major port town of Kristiansand. You'll turn south off of E-76 at Haukeligrend and wind up to Sessvatn at 3,000 feet. From here, road #12 takes you comfortably through ski resorts, past great steep mountains and much traditional architecture. The road is good and scenic. Skip the few smaller secondary routes. All along the valley you'll see the unique two-story *stabburs* (the top floor stored clothes; the bottom, food) and many sod roofs—even the bus stops have rooftops the local goats would love to munch.

This is a valley of traditional costumes, fiddlers, mouth organs, rose painting, whittling, and silversmiths. The famous Setesdal filigree echoes the rhythmical design of the Viking and medieval ages. But those zipping through will see little of this. The upper valley is dead in the summer and enjoys a bustling winter. Each town has a weekly rotating series of hikes and activities for the regular, stay-put-for-a-week visitor. What I'm getting at is that the charm of this valley isn't designed for 22 Days-style travel.

This is an easygoing stretch of sightseeing—nothing earthshaking. Let's just pretend you're on vacation and dilly-dally downhill all day long. Here are some interesting excuses to get out of the car:

Ekte Geitost—In the high country, just over the Sessvatn summit (3,000 ft.) you'll see goat herds and summer farms. If you see an "Ekte Geitost" sign, that means homemade goat cheese is for sale. (It's sold cheaper and in more manageable sizes in the grocery stores.) Some people think it looks like a decade's accumulation of ear wax. I think it's delicious. Remember, ekte means all-goat—real strong.

Dammar Vatnedalsvatn—Just south of Hovden is a two-mile side trip to a 400-foot-high rock pile dam. Great view, impressive rockery. They claim it's the highest dam in Northern Europe.

▲▲Bykle—The most interesting folk museum and church in Setesdal are in teeny Bykle. The seventeenth-century interior has two balconies—one for men and one for women (mid-June through mid-August, 10:00-17:00, 12:00-17:00 on Saturday and Sunday, 5 kr).

Bykle has a wonderful little open-air folk museum. The "Huldreheimen" Museum is a typical 800-year-old seter-house used when the cattle spent the summer high in the mountains. Follow the sign up a road to a farm high above the town, park, and hike a steep 150 yards into Norway's medieval peasant past—fine view, six houses filled with old stuff, good English information sheet. Open mid-June through mid-August, 10:00-18:00, Saturday-Sunday 12:00-18:00, 5 kr. Off-season, ask the friendly old lady who lives on the farm to let you take a look. Tel. 043/38101.

Grasbrokke—Just along the main road, at the Grasbrokke sign, on your left you'll see an old water mill (1630). A few minutes farther south is a Picnic and W.C. sign on the right. Exit onto that little road. You'll pass another old water mill. At the second picnic turnout (just before this roadlet returns to the highway, where you'll find a covered picnic table for rainy lunches), turn out and frolic along the river rocks.

Flateland—One mile east, off the main road, is the Setesdal museum (Rygnestadtunet), offering more of what you saw at Bykle (two buildings, daily from mid-June to mid-August 10:00-18:00 in July, 11:00-17:00 otherwise, 15 kr). Unless you're a glutton for culture, I wouldn't do both.

Valle—At Setesdal's prettiest village (but don't tell Bykle), you'll find a pleasant "husflid" shop (traditional homemade crafts and old-fashioned cooking, near the white church), fine silver and gold work at Grete and Ornulfs Sylvsmie, good traditional lunches in the cozy Bergtun Hotel (daily specials, 60 kr from 12:00-21:00), and a fine suspension bridge for little boys of any sex or age who still like to bounce and for anyone interested in a great view of the strange mountains over the river that look like polished petrified mud slides. European rock climbers tired of the overclimbed Alps often provide spectators with their sport. The TI is open mid-June through mid-August Monday-Friday 9:30-17:00, Saturday 9:30-20:00, closed Sundays, less in off-season, tel. 043/37312. (They sell boat tickets to Denmark.)

Nomeland—"Sylvartun," the silversmith with the valley's most aggressive publicity department, demonstrates the Setesdal specialty in a traditional log cabin from the seventeenth century. He gives a free fiddle concert most summer days at 14:00.

Grendi—The Ardal Church (1827) has a runestone in its yard, too. And for good measure, 300 yards south of the church is an oak tree said to be 900 years old.

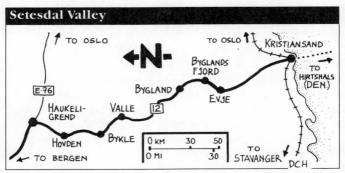

Setesdal Valley

TO OSLO

TO OSLO ↑ KRISTIANSAND

-N-

BYGLANDS FJORD

TO HIRTSHALS (DEN.)

E-76

BYGLAND

HAUKELI-GREND

VALLE 12

EVJE

HOVDEN

BYKLE

0 KM 30 50

0 MI 30

TO BERGEN

TO STAVANGER

DCH

Evje—A huge town by Setesdal standards (3,500 people), Evje is famous for its gems and mines. Fancy stones fill the shops here. Only rock hounds would find the nearby mines lots of fun (for a small fee you can hunt for gems). The Thulitten Stein (rock) and Souvenir Shop is just north of the town center, on a small road parallel to #12. There's a rock museum across the bridge on the south side of Evje (Evje og Hornnes museum, July-mid-August, 13:00-18:00, 15 kr). And a super new Setesdal Mineral-senter is planned for 1991, on the main road, three kilometers south of town. The road south from Evje to Kristiansand passes by a go-cart track and through a land of glassy lakes. It's a pleasant nonstop drive.

Setesdal—Kristiansand—Denmark

Kristiansand—This "capital of the south" with 60,000 inhabitants has a pleasant grid plan Renaissance layout (the Kvadraturen), a famous zoo with Norway's biggest amusement park (6 miles toward Oslo on E-18), and lots of big boats going to England and Denmark. It's the closest thing to a beach resort in Norway and a pleasant place to stroll through your last few hours in Norway before sailing to Denmark.

The "Kvadraturen" center around the bustling pedestrian market street is the shopping, eating, people-watching, and browsing town center. Walk along the Strand Promenaden (marina) and to the Christiansholm Fortress. You'll find plenty of Kafeterias, a Peppe's Pizza (open until 23:00, salad bar, on Gyldenloves), and budget

ethnic restaurants. For classy Norwegian dining with
classy Norwegians or just a beer with a view, visit the Sjo-
hoset (on the harbor at Ostre Strandgate 12). There are
two cinema complexes (6 screens, showing movies in
English, 40 kr, info at TI) within two blocks of the Fred
Olsen docks and the TI. (TI, Dronningengate 2, open
Monday-Friday, 8:00-18:00, Saturday 10:00-18:00, Sunday 13:00-18:00, off-season Monday-Friday 8:00-16:00
only. Tel. 042/26065.) The bank at the Fred Olsen terminal opens for each arrival and departure (even the midnight ones) and is reasonable. Norwegian money is used
on the boats.

Overnighting

Evje—Those who spend more time in Setesdal than they
planned can sleep in Evje. A wonderful *husrum* is in the
Alfred Falleras home (tel. 043/30086; their daughter,
across the street, speaks English at 043/30151). They have
just one room, but it's a huge suite sleeping from two to
four people. It rents for 200 kr plus 25 kr per person for
sheets. It's just north of the town center on the small road
that runs along #12, past the first speed bump ("sleeping
policeman" in Norwegian), across from the rock shop.
For more modern, bright, functional doubles, stay with
the **Haugen family**. For 260 kr, you get two bunks with
sheets (140 kr if you have sheets), pleasant garden, kitchenette, and a huge moose stuffed in the garage (on the
Arendal Road, last house on the left, see "rom" sign, tel.
043/30888).

Kristiansand—Far and away your best modern comfy
and cozy bet is the new **Hotel Sjoglott**. Friendly Tore
Kjostvedt gives his small hotel lots of class (450 doubles
with breakfast, near the harbor on a quiet street at Ostre
Strandgt 25, tel. 042/22120). Otherwise, Kristiansand
hotels are expensive and nondescript. The cheapest one,
the musty old **Bondeheimen** (tel. 042/24440) is 420 to
490 kr for a double with breakfast and shower. The
Hotel Norge (042/20000) is a little more modern and a
little more expensive with summer doubles for 560 kr.

The new youth hostel (042-95369) is cheap but not so central.

Sailing to Denmark

The Fred Olsen Line sails daily and nightly from Kristiansand to Hirtshals. The trip takes just over four hours (the overnight ride is slower), and there are up to three departures daily and a midnight to 6:30 crossing. Passengers pay about 160 kr and 220 kr for a car. This ride is nothing classy like the ride to Helsinki (Fred Olsen buys its boats used from other lines), but it's too cold to swim and you've got to get to Denmark somehow. There are decent smorgasbords. As soon as you're ready to commit yourself to a firm date, drop by a Norwegian travel agency to get your ticket and exact schedule information. Fred Olsen's information and reservation line is open daily 7:00-23:00; tel. 042/70501 in Kristiansand. Ask about specials. Prices go as low as 25 kr outside of peak and round-trip fares are often lower than one-way fares.

Sleep on the boat. I'd enjoy the evening in Kristiansand, board the night boat, and sail to Denmark while I sleep. Beds on board are reasonable. For around 80 kr you'll get a simple curtains-for-privacy couchette, for 130 kr a bed in a four-berth room, and for 160 kr per person, a private double with shower. You owe yourself this comfort if you're doing something as efficient as spending this night traveling. I slept so wekk, I missed the Denmark landing and crossed three times! After chewing me out, the captain said it happens a lot. Set your alarm or spend an extra day at sea.

While there's no problem getting on the boat and you're welcome to sprawl freely on the floor, or sit miserably in the "sleeperettes," cabins occasionally book up. Friday evening and Saturday and Monday mornings are most crowded. You can get a reservation for free and buy your ticket at the dock if you call Fred Olsen Lines.

JUTLAND, ARHUS, AND ACROSS DENMARK TO AERO

Sand dunes, Lego toys, fortified old towns, and moated manor houses, Jutland—the part of Denmark that's connected to the rest of Europe—is far from Copenhagen. After your boat docks, spend the morning in the wonderfully preserved old town of Arhus, Jutland's capital and Denmark's second largest city. By evening, after a long drive, you'll nestle into the quiet and quaint island of Aero.

Suggested Schedule	
7:00	Arrive in Hirtshals, Denmark, find breakfast.
8:00	Drive south to Arhus.
10:00	Tour Den Gamle By (the old town), picnic lunch.
14:00	Drive to Svendborg via Middelfart and Assens.
Evening	Catch the ferry to Aero, leaving your car in Svendborg.

Transportation

Denmark is a small country, but today you'll drive nearly its entire length—and that's a long way. From the dock in Hirtshals (you'll arrive very early), drive highway 13 to the freeway E-3, and continue south to Arhus. It's a two-hour drive even if you take the more scenic road 507 from Alborg (signs to Hadsund). Today's a very long day. You can breakfast on the ferry (50 kr) or along the way.

E-3 brings you right into central Arhus. Those skipping Arhus will skirt the center, turning right on Nordre Ringgade to follow E-3 south. To get to the Old Town, head into the center until you see signs to "Den Gamle By" which will lead you right there.

From Arhus you'll continue south on E-3 another 50

miles to E-66, where the Middlefart bridge takes you to
the Island of Fyn (Funen in English). At Odense take
Highway 9 to Svendborg.

Leave your car in Svendborg at the easy long-term
parking lot two blocks from the ferry dock and sail for
the little isle of Aero. The Svendborg—Aeroskobing ferry
is a pleasant one-hour crossing (175 kr round-trip per car,
78 kr round-trip per person). There are only five boats a
day (7:45, 11:00, 14:40, 17:40 and 21:00, but double
check), and while walk-ons always make it on, cars need
reservations (tel. 62521018). The town of Aeroskobing is
tiny: everything is just a few cobbles from the ferry landing. Remember, it's wise, especially in this age of over-
booking, to call and reconfirm your flight home 72 hours
before departure (SAS tel. 31 54 17 01, in Copenhagen).

Arhus

Denmark's second-largest city (pop. 260,000), Arhus is
the cultural hub of Jutland. Its Viking founders, ever con-
scious of aesthetics, chose a lovely wooded where-the-
river-hits-the-sea setting, and today it bustles with a
lively port and an important university. It's well worth a
stop. The Arhus Tourist Office is in the town hall (tel. 86
12 16 00, open daily 9:00-22:00, mid-June through
August, shorter hours and closed Sundays in other
months). Ideally, you picked up the very helpful Arhus
tourist information brochure and map in Copenhagen. If
not, get it here. They run a fine city introductory bus tour
(daily in the summer at 10:00 for 2 ½ hours from the TI)
for 30 kr. That tour ticket also gives you 24 hours of
unlimited city bus travel.

Sightseeing Highlights—Arhus

▲▲▲**Den Gamle By**— "The Old Town" open-air folk
museum puts Arhus on the touristic map. This is a unique
gathering of 65 half-timbered houses and crafts shops, all
wonderfully furnished just like when they were new
back in the days of Hans Christian Andersen. The
"Mayor's House" from 1597 is the nucleus and reason
enough to visit. Unlike other Scandinavian open-air
museums, which focus on rural folk life, Den Gamle By
re-creates old Danish town life. (35 kr entry, there are
enough English descriptions to make the guidebook
unnecessary, open daily June through August, 9:00 to
18:00, May and September 10:00-17:00, with shorter
hours off-season, daily walking tour at 15:00, take bus #3
to the "Old Town," tel. 86 12 31 88.) The buildings are
locked, but it's a peaceful park after hours.

▲**Forhistorisk Museum Moesard**—This prehistory
museum at Moesgard, just south of Arhus, is famous for
its incredibly well preserved Grauballe Man. This 2,000-
year-old "bog man" looks like a fellow half his age. He's
amazingly intact. You'll see his skin, nails, hair, and even
the slit in his throat that they gave him at the sacrificial
banquet. The museum has fine Viking and Stone, Bronze

and Iron Age exhibits. 20 kr. Open daily 10:00-17:00, closed Mondays in the off-season. Take bus #6 from the Arhus station to the last stop. Behind the museum, a pre-historic open-air museum ("trackway") stretches two miles down to a fine beach (good 10 kr guidebooklet) where, in the summer, bus #19 takes you back down-town. The museum cafeteria sells picnics to go if you're in the mood.

Arhus Cathedral—Denmark's biggest at over 300 feet long and tall, this late Gothic (from 1479) church is open to tourists daily except Sundays from 9:30-16:00 (shorter hours off-season).

Other Arhus attractions—There's lots more to see and do in Arhus including an art museum, a Viking museum (free, in a bank basement across from the cathedral), and a "Tivoli" amusement park. Two-hour walking tours through the old center and the Viking museum are given summer Thursdays at 14:00 from the TI (25 kr). A popular "Meet the Danes" program puts interested visitors in touch with locals for an evening of talk, coffee, and cake. This is arranged through the TI (at least a day in advance).

Accommodations in Arhus
Missionshotellet Ansgar—This huge traditional hotel at 14 Banegardsplads, near the town hall, charges from 465 to 590 kr for doubles with breakfast. Tel. 86 12 41 22.
Ericksen's Hotel—This is a clean and very simple shower-down-the-hall place, also very central, with doubles for around 320 kr. Banegardsplads 6-8, tel. 86 13 62 96.

The TI can set you up in a private home for around 100 kr per person. They also have summer deals on ritzy hotels that can match the prices of the two dull listings above. Also, the local **Youth Hotel** is a good one, situated near the water two miles out of town on Ostreskovvej, tel. 86 16 72 98, bus #1, #6, #9, or #16 to the end and fol-low the signs.

The **Sleep In** is an alternative culture center offering the cheapest beds in town near the cathedral. It's your basic mattress on the floor for 55 kr. Cheap meals and

rental blankets, open July and August. Mejlgade 53, tel.
86 19 22 55.

Other Jutland Sights

Jutland is the large chunk of Denmark that is attached to
Germany. The rest of the country consists of islands. The
land of the Jutes has vast beaches, lots of sand dunes,
forests, soft hills, rather desolate moors, and a few interesting sights. Arhus is the only blockbuster sight, but
here are a few others to consider.

▲▲**Legoland**—Legoland is Scandinavia's top kids' sight.
If you have one (or think you might be one), it's a fun
stop. Thirty-three million Lego bricks (European tinker
toys) are creatively arranged into Mt. Rushmore, the
Parthenon, "Mad" Ludwig's castle, the Statue of Liberty,
wild animals, and so on, and combined with lots of rides,
restaurants, trees, and smiles into one big park. It's a Lego
world here, as everything is cleverly related to this very
popular toy. Surprisingly, however, the restaurants don't
serve "Legolamb." The park has a great doll collection
and a toy museum full of mechanical wonders from the
early 1900s, many ready to jump into action as soon as
you push the button. There's a Lego playroom for some
hands-on fun for your kids—and a campground across
the street if they refuse to move on. East of E-3 on highway 28, one hour from Arhus or Odense in the otherwise
unremarkable town of Billund. Open May through mid-
September 10:00 to 21:00 daily, closed off-season, tel. 75
33 13 33. 40 kr entry, 20 kr for kids; special price for 8
rides, 28 kr.

If you're sleeping in nearby Billund, try **Eva and Egon
Jorgensen**, 200 kr per double, 30 kr for breakfast, Kol-
dingvej 1 (left at the corner where road 28 crosses the
road to Legoland), tel. 75 33 10 46. Or, **Anna and Victor
Christensen**, 250 kr per double, Systemvej 25, Billund,
tel. 75 33 15 68.

Jelling—If you've always wanted to see the hometown
of the ancient Danish kings, Gorm the Old and Harold
Bluetooth, this is your chance. Jelling is a small village (12
miles from Legoland, just off E-3 near Vejle) with a small

church that has Denmark's oldest frescoes and two very old runic stones in its courtyard—often called "Denmark's birth certificate."

▲**Ribe**—A Viking port a thousand years ago, Ribe is the oldest and possibly loveliest town in Denmark. An entertaining mix of cobbled lanes and leaning old houses with a fine church (5 kr, bright modern paintings under old Romanesque arches). A smoky, low-ceiling, very atmospheric inn, the Weis Stue, serves great meals across the street from the church. Drop by the TI for its handy walking tour brochure, or better yet, catch one of the guided town walks (daily, 11:30, 20 kr).

▲▲▲**Aero**—This small (22-by-6-mile) island on the south edge of Denmark is salty and sleepy as can be. Tombstones here say things like, "Here lies Christian Hansen at anchor with his wife. He'll not weigh until he stands before God." It's the kind of island where baskets of new potatoes sit in front of houses—for sale on the honor system. Being about ten miles across the water from Germany, you'll see plenty of smug Germans who return regularly to this peaceful retreat.

Aeroskobing is Aero's town in a bottle. Temple Fielding said it's "one of five places in the world that you must see." It's the only entirely protected town in Denmark. Drop into the 1680s, when Aeroskobing was the wealthy homeport of over a hundred windjammers. The many Danes who come here for the tranquillity—washing up the cobbled main drag in waves with the landing of each boat—call it the "fairy tale town." The very Danish word for the atmosphere here is *hyggelig*—cozy.

The Tourist Office (several blocks up from the ferry on Torvet, open in summer Monday-Friday 10:00-17:00, Saturday 9:00-13:00, Sunday 10:00-12:00, tel. 62 52 13 00), can find you a room in a private home (doubles for 170 kr).

On arrival, reserve your ferry out (if you drive a car), tel. 62 52 10 18. The only real English guide-type information, with a good map and a town walking tour, is in the red "Aero Rundt" booklet (15 kr in most shops).

Accommodations

Pension Vestergade—Phyllis Packnass runs this pleasantly quirky old place (built for a sea captain's daughter in 1784) located right on the main street in the town center. She takes very good care of her guests with a homey TV room and a library with Aero guidebooks you can use. (225 kr per double, 260 kr for doubles with a kitchen, breakfast is extra, good discount for 3-night stays, loft rooms have great views, climb upstairs to snoop around. Ask to borrow a bike. Picnic in the backyard or upstairs. Vestergade 44, 5970 Aeroskobing, tel. 62 52 22 98.) This is your ideal home on Aero.

   Det Lille Hotel—Friendly and chatty Erling and Lise Jensen run this former nineteenth-century captain's home. It's warm, tidy, and modern—like a sailboat. Their six rooms (340 kr per double, 205 per single) include a huge breakfast and loaner bikes. Open April-November. Just one street off the harbor at Smedegade 33, next to the cutest house in town, 5970 Aeroskobing, tel. 62 52 23 00.

   There are several very peaceful bed and breakfasts in the countryside. **Julie Hansen** (180 kr doubles, breakfast extra, Ostermarksvej 20, west of Aeroskobing, tel. 62 52 24 25) is the only one who speaks English.

   The **Aeroskobing Youth Hostel** is a glorious place, equipped with a fine living room, members' kitchen, and family rooms with two or four beds (55 kr each). The place is usually full from mid-June through mid-August and closed from October through March (500 yards out of town at Smedevejen 13, tel. 62 52 10 04).

   Dunkaer Kro—Set quietly far from town in the center of the island, this traditional old inn with great food, a classy dining room, and a rowdy pub has basic doubles with down quilts for 275 kr, breakfast extra. 5981 Dunkaer, tel. 62 52 15 54.

   Camping—This three-star campground (follow the waterfront, a short walk from the center) is on a fine beach, has a lodge with a fireplace, windsurfing, and cottages (without bedding) for 4 people for 70 kr plus 35 kr

per person or 65 kr more with a kitchenette. It's open
from May through mid-September and always has room
for campers (35 kr each). Tel. 62 52 18 54.

Eating in Aero
Okay, the truth is that without tourism, this island has no
economy. The eateries are touristic. Only picnicking is
cheap. But good values do hide out. My favorite places
are on or near the top of Vestergade (near Pension Vestergade). **Madam Bla's coffeehouse** (Vestergade 39) is best
with delicious candlelit-cuddly or garden-cheery meals
for 100 kr. **MUMM's** candlelit ambience is occasionally
blown out by the German yachting crowd, but the food
is fine and reasonable (Sondergade 12). Up Vestergade is
the light and lovable little **Bog Cafe** and the dark and
drinkable **Landbogarden**, depending on your mood. A
$3 dinner? The bakery next to Bog Cafe—homemade
bread, cheese, a tin of liver paste, and a liter of drink
yogurt. The home-made waffle cones in the pink shop
across the street from the Vestergade Pension are stom-
pin' good.

The only real late night action is the Friday and Saturday night disco at the **Strandskoven Restaurant** (next
to the campground, very late).

THE ISLE OF AERO

After the staggering beauty of Norway's fjord country and all you've seen so far, the sleepy isle of Aero is the cuddle after the climax. It's the perfect time-passed world in which to wind down, enjoy the seagulls, and take a bike ride. Today is yours. By the end of it, you'll wish you had another. Pedal a rented bike into the essence of Denmark. Lunch in a traditional kro country inn. Settle in a cobbled world of sailors who, after someone connected a steam engine to a propeller, decided "maybe building ships in bottles is more my style."

Suggested Schedule

Morning	Sleep in.
10:00	Bike tour with picnic or lunch at the traditional Dunkaer Kro Inn.
15:00	Explore little Aeroskobing, pop into the Bottled Ship museum and Hammerlich House museum.

Sightseeing Highlights
▲▲▲The Town of Aeroskobing—It's just a pleasant place to wander. Stubby little porthole-type houses lean on each other like drunk but sleeping sailors, cast iron gas lights still shine each evening, the harbor now caters to holiday yachts, and on midnight low tides you can almost hear the crabs playing cards. Snoop around. It's okay. Notice all the snooping mirrors on the houses. Antique locals may be following your every move.

The town economy, once rich with the windjammer trade, hit the rocks in the twentieth century. Outside of tourism, there are few jobs. The kids from 15 to 18 years old go to a boarding school in Svendborg. Few return. It's an interesting discussion, do the island folk pickle their culture in tourism or forget about the cuteness and get modern? This town is a favorite among Danes.

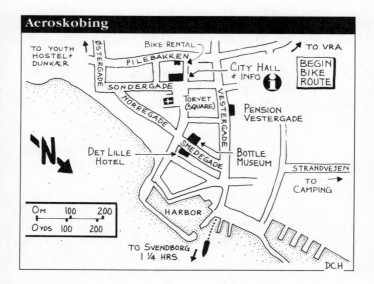

▲The Hammerich House is 12 funky rooms in 3 houses filled with 200- to 300-year-old junk (daily in the summer from 10:00 to 12:00 and 13:00 to 15:00, Tuesday and Friday open 19:00-21:00 also, 10 kr).

▲The "Bottle Peter" museum on Smedegade is a fascinating house of 750 different bottled ships. Old Peter Jacobsen bragged that he drank the contents of each bottle except those containing milk. He died in 1960 (most likely buried in a glass coffin), leaving a lifetime of tedious little creations for us visitors to marvel at (daily 11:00-17:00 from May-September, 10:00-16:00 otherwise, 10 kr). The third sight in town, the Aero museum, is nowhere near as interesting as the Hammerich House.

▲▲▲The Aero Island bike ride (or car tour if you prefer)— This 18-mile trip will show you the best of this windmill-covered island's nuclear charms. While the highest point on the island is only 180 feet, the wind can be strong and the hills seem long. This ride is good exercise. If your hotel can't loan you a bike (ask), rent one from the Esso Station (Pilebaekken 7, tel. 62 52 11 10, go through the green door to the right of the TI, past the public WC and garden to the next road, ask for their free "cykel map," 30 kr for one-speeds, 35 kr for three-speeds— about the best 5 kr you could spend on this island). The youth hostel and the campground also rent bikes. On Aero there are no deposits and few locks. If you leave in the morning, you'll hit the Kro Inn in time for lunch. Ready to go? "May the wind always be at your back, and if it's not . . . make some."

Leave Aeroskobing to the west on the road to Vra. You'll see the first of many U-shaped farms, typical of this island. The three sides block the wind and are used for storing cows, hay, and people. "Gaard" (meaning "farm") shows up on many local names. Until the old generation's gone, you'll see only sturdy old women behind the wheelbarrows. Bike along the coast in the protection of the dyke that made the once-salty swampland to your left farmable. You'll see a sleek modern windmill and, soon, a pleasant cluster of mostly modern summer cottages called Borgnaes. (At this point, wimps can take a shortcut directly to Vindeballe.)

Keep to the right, pass another Vindeballe turnoff, go along a secluded beach, and then climb uphill over the island's 180-foot summit to Bregninge. Unless you're tired of thatched and half-timbered cottages, turn right and roll through Denmark's "second longest village" to the church. Take a peek inside. (Great pulpit for frustrated preachers and photo hams, public WC in the church yard.) Then roll back through Bregninge past many more U-shaped "gaards," heading about a mile down the main road to Vindeballe, taking the Voderup exit.

A straight road leads you downhill (with a jog to the right) to a rugged bluff called Voderup Klint. If I were a pagan, I'd worship here—the sea, the wind, the chilling view, Germany in the distance. Notice how the land slipped in long chunks to make terraces steppping down to the sea. Hike down to the foamy beach. While the wind can drag a kite flier at the top, the beach can be ideal for sunbathing.

Then it's on to Tanderup. You'll roll past the old farm full of cows, a lovely pond, and right past a row of wind-

Aero Island Bike Route

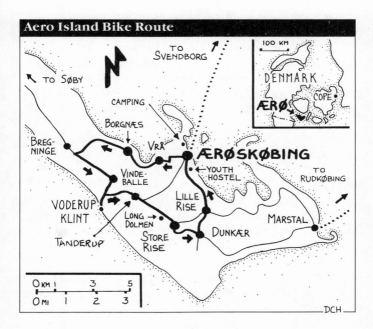

bent stumps. (Care to guess the direction of the prevailing wind?) Follow the sign to Tanderup, stay parallel to the big road through the town, past a lovely farm that does bed and breakfast, the potato stand, and finally to the main road. Turn right. At the Aeroskobing turnoff, just before the tiny little white house, turn left to the big stone (commemorating the return of the island to Denmark from Germany in 1750). Seattle-ites should be sure to visit Claus Clausen's rock (in the picnic area), a memorial to an extremely obscure Washington state pioneer.

Return to the big road, pass the little white house, and head toward Store Rise, the next church spire in the distance. Just after the Stokkeby turnoff, follow the very rough tree-lined path on your right to the Tingstedet Long Dolmen, just behind the church spire. Here you'll see a 5,000-year-old early neolithic burial place, often guarded by the megalithic lamb. Aero had over a hundred of these prehistoric tombs, but few survive.

Carry on down the lane to the Store Rise church. Inside, notice the little boats hanging in the nave, the fine altarpiece, and Martin Luther keeping his Protestant hand on the rudder in the stern. Can you find anyone buried in the graveyard whose name doesn't end in "sen"? Continue down the main road with the impressive—and hopeful—forest of modern windmills on your right until you get to Dunkaer.

Hungry? There's a fine little bakery just down the Marstal road. Or for a traditional splurge, lunch at the Dunkaer "Kro" Inn. Have beer and a sandwich (40 kr) or go for a "Frokost platter" (60 kr if you ask for the "light budget education in Danish cuisine" version). Remember the art of open-face sandwiches: herring first, then meat, both on dark bread, finishing with cheese on white bread. Do it elegant and dainty, one slice with your topping, eaten with fork and knife—pinky out.

For the home stretch, take the small road, signed Lille Rise, past the topless windmill. Except for "Lille Rise," it's all downhill from here as you coast past great sea views back home to Aeroskobing.

Still rolling? Bike out past the campground, along the strand (beach) to poke into the coziest little beach houses you'll never see back in the "big is beautiful" U.S.A. This is Europe, where the concept of sustainability is neither new or subversive.

ODENSE, ROSKILDE, AND BACK TO COPENHAGEN

Okay, enough resting. You'd think this was a vacation or something. Let's have one last flurry of sightseeing activity as we return to Copenhagen. Catch the early ferry—breakfast on board—to get to Odense, home of Hans Christian Andersen and Odense's fine open-air folk museum. Roskilde, with its great Viking ships and cathedral, is the last stop before you find yourself back where you started—in Copenhagen.

Suggested Schedule

Day 21

6:20	Breakfast on the early ferry.
7:40	Pick up your car in Svendborg and drive to Odense.
8:30	Tour Hans Christian Andersen's home and the Montergarden Urban History museum.
13:00	Picnic on the Knudshoved-Halsskov ferry from Funen to Zealand (one hour) and drive to Roskilde (another hour).
15:00	Tour Roskilde's Viking ships and cathedral.
18:00	Drive "home" to Copenhagen where your room is reserved and waiting.

Day 22

Fly home to the United States from Copenhagen.

Transportation: Aero—Copenhagen

Today we need to catch the early (6:20) ferry back to Svendborg. Call 62 52 10 18 for information. Reservations for walk-ons are never necessary. On Saturday and Sunday, there are normally no early trips. By 7:40, you'll be driving north on Highway 9; follow signs first to Faborg, past the Egeskov castle to Odense. If you're doing the folk museum, leave Route 9 just south of town at Hojby, turning left toward Dalum and the Odense Campground (on Odensveg). Look for Den Fynske Landsby signs (near the train tracks, south edge of town). After touring the open-air folk museum, drive into the center. If you're going directly to fairy tale land, drive into town and follow the signs to H. C. Andersen Hus. If you go direct, parking will be simple on the street near the H.C. Andersen Hotel. Drop into the hotel to get the free and excellent Odense map/guide. Everything's dead until 9:00. There's coffee in the hotel or buy your picnic on Overgade street.

Leave Odense following signs for E-20 and Nyborg. The freeway passes Nyborg and butts right up to the Knudshoved-Halsskov ferry (always call for free reservation at 33 14 88 80, one-hour crossing, boats leave every 40 minutes). Signs will take you to Roskilde, leaving the freeway at Ringsted. Set your sights on the twin church spires and park somewhere between there and the water, where you'll find the Viking ships.

Copenhagen is just 30 minutes from Roskilde. If you're returning your car to the airport, stay on E-20 to the bitter end, following signs to Kobenhavn C and then to Kastrup Airport. From there a city bus will take you downtown and to the hotel you reserved about 22 days ago.

Sightseeing Highlights

▲**Odense**—Founded in 988, named after the Nordic Zeus, Odin, and important economically only in the nineteenth century when a canal enabled it to become the port city of the garden island's produce, Odense is famous today basically for its hometown storyteller, Hans Christian Andersen. Andersen once said, "Perhaps Odense will one day become famous because of me and perhaps people from many countries will travel to Odense because of me." Today Odense, pronounced "OH en za," is one of Denmark's most visited towns. Denmark's third largest city, with 170,000 people, it's big and industrial. But its old center retains some of the fairy tale charm it had in the days of H.C.A. and has plenty to offer.

Park your car and hoof it. It is well connected to Copenhagen by train-boat-train (sixteen 3-hour trips each day).
The TI is in the town hall right downtown (tel. 66 12 75
20, open daily in summer 9:00-19:00, Sunday 11:00-19:00,
off-season Monday-Friday 9:00-17:00, Saturday 9:00-
12:00). They run city bus tours and a "Meet the Danes"
program. But for a quick visit, all you need is the map/
guide free from the HCA Hotel next to the HCA Hus.

▲**Den Fynske Landsby**—The Funen Village Open-Air
Museum is a sleepy gathering of 24 old buildings preserv-
ing the eighteenth-century culture of this region. There
are no explanations in the buildings because the many
school groups who visit play guessing games. So pick up
the 15 kr guidebook. 15 kr admission, open June-August
daily from 9:00-18:30; April-May and September-
October daily from 9:00-16:00. Off-season, open only
Sundays from 10:00-16:00, tel. 66 13 13 72. From mid-
July to mid-August, there are H. C. Andersen plays in the
theater every afternoon (the 30 kr ticket includes admission 90 minutes early to see the museum).

▲▲**Hans Christian Andersen Hus**—This museum is
packed with mementos from the popular writer's life, his
many letters and books, and hordes of children and
tourists. It's fun if you like his tales. At Hans Jensens-
straede 39, open daily in summer 9:00-18:00, shorter
hours off-season. 20 kr admission. Things are explained
well in English, so the guidebook is unnecessary. Across
the street is a popular shop full of imaginative mobiles
and Danish arts and crafts.

▲▲▲**Montergarden Urban History and Culture
Museum**—Very close to the H.C.A. Hus (near the H.C.A.
Hotel), this fun little museum offers a good look at
Odense history, early photos, a great coin collection, a
town lane re-created, a Nazi occupation exhibit, and the
cheapest coffee in Denmark (2 kr). Nothing's in English,
and it's so interesting you'll wish it was, so pick up the 10
kr guidebook. Overgade 48, tel. 66 13 13 72, open
10:00-16:00 daily.

Brandt's Klaedefabrik—In 1977 a huge textile factory
(18,000 sq. meters) was shut down. Rather than demolish

it, they turned it into a cultural center. Today it houses
several modern art and graphics and printing museums,
shops, and cafes. The people-watching is great from its
outdoor cafes.

Egeskov Castle—One of Denmark's most impressive
castles is newly opened to the public. Egeskov shows off
its royal and very lived-in interior and its fine gardens. If
you're a fan of fuchsias, old cars, or hunting trophies, this
place is thrilling. Expensive—50 kr. Open May-September
10:00-17:00, tel. 62 27 10 16, just off the Odense-Svendborg
road. Bus connections are bad, but it's very easy to reach
by car.

▲**Roskilde**—Denmark's roots—Viking and royal—are
on display in Roskilde, a pleasant town 20 miles west of
Copenhagen. Five hundred years ago, Roskilde was Denmark's leading city. Today, the town that introduced
Christianity to Denmark in A.D. 980 is most famous for
hosting northern Europe's biggest rock/jazz/folk festival
(ten days early in each July). Wednesday and Saturday are
flea/flower/produce market days. Its TI next to the cathedral (tel. 42 35 27 00) is helpful. Roskilde is an easy side
trip from Copenhagen on the S-Tog commuter train.

▲▲**Roskilde Cathedral**—Roskilde's imposing twelfth-
century, twin-spired cathedral houses the tombs of 38
Danish kings and queens. It's a stately, modern-looking
old church with great marble work, paintings (notice the
impressive 3-D painting, with Christian IV looking like a
pirate, in the room behind the small pipe organ), and
wood carvings in and around the altar and the silly little
glockenspiel (that plays high above the entrance on the
top of every hour). It's all surrounded by an impressive
sea of clean cobbles (except for rice in the cracks). The 20
kr guidebook is very good. April-September 9:00-17:45,
off-season 10:00-16:00, Sundays from 12:30, 3 kr admission. Toward the sea from the church is a wild field that
protects the remains of the medieval town. It's a pleasant
walk down to the harbor and Viking ships.

▲▲▲**Viking Ship Museum (Vikingeskibshallen)**—
This award-winning museum displays five different Viking ships—one is like the boat Leif Ericsson sailed to

America a thousand years ago, another is like those depicted in the Bayeux Tapestry. The descriptions are excellent—and in English. It's the kind of museum where you want to read everything. Buy the 2 kr guide booklet and request the English movie introduction as you enter. These ships were deliberately sunk to block a nearby harbor and only recently excavated, preserved, and pieced together. The museum cafeteria serves the original Viking-burger (26 kr)—great after a hard day of pillage, plunder, or sightseeing. Open April-October 9:00-17:00, November-March 10:00-16:00, tel. 42 35 65 65, 20 kr entry.

▲**Ancient Sights near Roskilde**—One of the best ancient sights in Denmark is the 5,000-year-old passage grave near the village of Om (just off Route 14). Bring a flashlight—or matches for the candles people have put on the walls. You'll actually be able to stand up in this grave site surrounded by 15 wall stones and under 4 large ceiling stones.

Lejre Research Centre—This well-publicized "Iron Age Community" is an intriguing prehistoric "camp" but not worth the time or steep admission price (35 kr, 10:00-17:00 May-September, tel. 42 38 02 45).

Chieftains Tomb—Near the town of Lejre is a desolate burial ground consisting of two rows of stones that form a Viking ship. Take the very tiny road at the edge of Gamle Lejre where you see the "Skibsaetningen" sign. All of these sights and others are explained with a good map in the "Surroundings of Roskilde" brochure, available at tourist offices.

Copenhagen

It'll feel fine to be back "home" in Copenhagen. Depending on how much time you have left, there's lots more to do in Copenhagen. For departure and airport tips, refer back to the Day 1 pages.

Congratulations! You've completed the circle. Soon you'll be home browsing through your photos, and this trip will be stored away in the slide carousel of your mind. But before too long you'll find yourself scheming about another faraway adventure.

Scandinavia in 22 days by train is most efficient with a little reworking as shown in the following itinerary. You
also have a few options that drivers don't. If you sleep on
the very comfortable Nordic trains, places not worth
driving to on a short trip become feasible. Consider a
swing through Finland's eastern lakes district or the scenic ride to Trondheim.

I'd go overnight whenever possible on any ride six or
more hours long. Consider streamlining your plan by
doing North Zealand sights as a side trip from Copenhagen, skipping the Vaxjo-Kalmar day, and spending the
night on the very efficient Copenhagen-Stockholm train
(there is no Copenhagen-Kalmar overnight train). The
Bergen-Setesdal-Arhus-Copenhagen leg is possible on
public transit, but getting from Bergen to Kristiansand
will really test your patience and Setesdal is not worth the
trouble if you don't have the poke-around freedom a car
gives you. A flight straight home from Bergen would be
wonderfully efficient. Otherwise return via the scenic
Bergen-Oslo run. It's about 20 hours by train from Bergen to Copenhagen via Oslo.

The suggested train itinerary is heavy on fjord scenery
(my kind of problem). You'll find the Andalsnes-Flam
segment trying but worthwhile. Fjord country buses,
boats, and trains connect but not without lengthy one- to
three-hour layovers. "Norway in a Nutshell" is an excep-
tion. The Aurland-Bergen boat, which is too expensive
for drivers, is a great fjord finale.

Scandinavia in 22 Days by Train

Day	Place	Overnight in
1	Arrive in Copenhagen	Copenhagen
2	Sightsee Copenhagen	Copenhagen
3	Copenhagen, side trip to North Zealand	Copenhagen
4	Copenhagen, Roskilde, Odense, Aero	Aeroskobing
5	Aeroskobing	Aeroskobing
6	Aero-Copenhagen-Vaxjo, Sweden	Vaxjo
7	Vaxjo, glass country, Kalmar	night train
8	Stockholm	Stockholm
9	Stockholm, side trip to Uppsala	boat
10	Helsinki	Helsinki
11	Helsinki, Turku	boat
12	Stockholm	night train
13	Oslo	Oslo
14	Oslo	Oslo
15	Lillehammer, Gudbrandsdal, Andalsnes	Andalsnes
16	"Golden Route," Geiranger Fjord	Hellesylt
17	Fjord country to Flam	Aurland
18	"Norway in a Nutshell"	Aurland
19	Boat to Bergen through Sognefjord	Bergen
20	Bergen	Bergen
21	Bergen-to-Oslo scenic train	night train
22	Copenhagen	

Below are the basic connections you'll need to do Scandinavia by train, bus, and boat (they work in both directions). Some lines make fewer runs or even close in the off-season. This information is all you need to plan your trip. Pick up exact schedules as you travel, available free at any tourist office. The trip I've laid out easily justifies the purchase of a 21-day Nord-tourist pass ($350 first class, $250 second class, buy at any Scandinavian station) or a 21-day Eurailpass ($498, first class only, from travel agents in U.S. only).

The Eurailpass covers all the train rides listed plus the
boats from Stockholm to Helsinki and Turku, the
Denmark-Sweden ferry, and the Halsskov-Knudshoved
ride. The Nordtourist pass is good on all of these (except
the Stockholm-Helsinki ride, only 50%), plus all Danish
state ferries and the Kristiansand-Hirtshals trip. Your
travel agent has brochures and more information.

	Departure/ day	Hours
Kobenhavn to:		
Hillerod (Frederiksborg)	40	½
Louisiana (Helsinger train to Humlebaek)	40	½
Roskilde	16	½, on Odense train
Odense	16	3
Helsingor (ferry to Sweden) tel. 33 14 88 80	40	½
Stockholm	6-8	8
Vaxjo via Alvesta	6	5
Oslo	4	10
Berlin via Gedser	2	9
Amsterdam	2	11
Frankfurt/Rhine castles	4	10
Hamburg	5	5 ½
Stockholm to:		
Kalmar	6 (1 night train)	8
Helsinki	2	14
Turku	2	10
Uppsala	30	¾
Oslo	3	7
Vaxjo to glassworks	TI tour or side trip by bus	
Vaxjo to Kalmar	9	1 ½
Helsinki to Turku	7	2 ½
Oslo to:		
Lillehammer	4	2 ½
Andalsnes	3	6 ½
Bergen	4	7-8
Trondheim	3	7-8

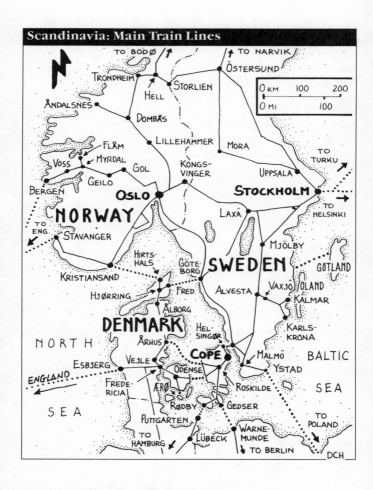

Scandinavia: Main Train Lines

Norway's Mountain and Fjord Country
Lillehammer to:

Andalsnes	4	4
Lom (change at Otta)	3	4
Andalsnes to Alesund by bus (with each arriving train)		
	2	½
Andalsnes over Trollstigvegen		
to Geiranger Fjord	4	early each morning

Lom to Sogndal (bus departures 8:50 and 15:50)	2	4 (summer)
Sogndal to Kaupanger	10	½
Sogndal to Gudvangen	4	3
Flam to Bergen via Myrdal	3	3 ½
Flam to Bergen by boat (departs 6:00, 15:05	2	6 ½ , $50
Flam-Aurland-Gudvangen by boat	3	2
Gudvangen to Voss (stop at Stalheim)	7	1 ¼ by bus

Kaupanger to:

Gudvangen (departures 8:50, 11:40, 14:45, 17:40)	4	2 ¼
Revsnes	16	¼
Flam/Aurland	4	2

Bergen to:

Haukelegrend, one trip possible daily, several changes, complicated

Alesund	1	10

South Norway

Setesdal Valley, Hovden to Kristiansand	2	5

Kristiansand to:

Oslo	6	4-5
Hirtshals, Denmark by ferry	4	4, longer overnight

Denmark

Hirtshals to Arhus	16	2 ½
Arhus to Odense	16	2
Odense to Svendborg	16	1
Svendborg to Aero, ferry	5 (summer)	1 ¼
Aero to Kobenhavn	5	5
Halsskov-Knudshoved	26	1
tel. 33 14 88 80		

TELEPHONING AND TOURIST INFORMATION

Too many timid tourists never figure out the phones. They work and are essential to smart travel. Call hotels in advance to make a reservation whenever you know when you'll be in town. If there's a language problem, ask someone at your hotel to talk to your next hotel for you.

Public phone booths are much cheaper than using the more convenient hotel phones. The key to dialing direct is understanding area codes. For calls to other European countries, dial the international access code, followed by the country code, followed by the area code without its zero, and finally the local number. When dialing long distance within a country, start with the area code (including its zero), then the local number. (In Denmark, all numbers, local or long distance, are eight digits and have no area code.)

Telephoning the United States from a pay phone is easy. Gather a pile of large coins ($2.50 or 15 kr per minute) and find a booth. The best budget approach is to call with a coin and have that person return your call at a specified time at your hotel. From the U.S.A. they'd dial 011-country code-area code without zero-local number. Collect and person-to-person calls are more expensive and complicated. Calls from midnight to 8:00 a.m. are 20% cheaper, but Scandinavia to U.S.A. calls are twice as expensive as direct calls from the U.S.A. Major telephone credit cards make phoning home even easier. With my AT&T card I just dial the local access number (listed below), tell the American operator the number I'm calling and my card number, and I'm billed at the cheaper American rate plus about a $2.50 service charge per call. Major city train stations have impressive telecommunications centers.

Country Codes
U.S.A. and Canada—1
Great Britain—44
Germany—49
Denmark—45
Finland—358
Norway—47
Sweden—46

International Access Codes
(to call out of . . .)
Denmark—009
Finland—990
Norway—095
Sweden—009
U.S.A.—011

U.S. Embassies or Consulates

Copenhagen—31 42 31 44
Helsinki—90/171931
Oslo—02/566880
Stockholm—08/630520

AT&T Access Code

8001-0010
9800-100-10
050-12-011
020-795-611

Emergency	Local Dir. Assist.	Intl. Dir. Assist.
Denmark—000	0033	0039
Norway—002	0180	0181
Sweden—90000	07975	0019

Tourist Information Numbers

City	Area Code	TI
Copenhagen		33111325, 33156518
Vaxjo	0470	41410
Kalmar	0480	15350
Stockholm	08	7892000, 240880
Helsinki	90	174088, 1693-757
Uppsala	018	117500, 161825
Oslo	02	171124, 427170
Lillehammer	062	59299
Lom	062	11286
Gaupne (Nigard)	056	81211
Andalsnes	072	21622
Aurland (Flam)	056	33313
Bergen	05	321480
Setesdal (Hovden)	043	39630
Setesdal (Valle)	043	37312
Kristiansand	042	26065
Arhus		86121600
Odense		66127520
Aeroskobing		62521300
Roskilde		42352700

Tourist Information (TI)

Each of these countries has an excellent network of tourist information offices both locally and in the U.S.A. Before your trip, send a letter to each country's National Tourist Office (listed below) telling them of your general plans and asking for information. They'll send you the general packet, and if you ask for specifics (calendars of local festivals, good hikes around Bergen, castle hotels in Jutland, and so on), you may get an impressive amount of help. If you have a specific problem, they are a good source of assistance.

During your trip, your first stop in each town should be the tourist office, where you'll take your turn at the informational punching bag smiling behind the desk. This person is rushed and tends to be robotic. Prepare. Have a list of questions and a proposed plan to double-check with him or her. They have a wealth of material that the average "Duh, do you have a map?" tourist never taps. If you'll be arriving late, or want to arrange a room, call ahead. If you arrive in a town when the TI is closed, or a town without one, the biggest hotel in town will normally have a free map/info brochure. By the way, you can get some impressive scrapbook photos, charts, and maps from the local TIs.

A quick visit to each country's national tourist office in Copenhagen will allow you to pick up city maps and information that will save you untold hassles over the course of your trip.

In the U.S.A., write to Norway, Sweden, Denmark, or Finland c/o Scandinavian Tourist Board, 655 3rd Ave., New York, NY 10017, or call (212) 949-2333.

SCANDINAVIAN PHRASES

English	Danish	Norwegian	Swedish
Engelsk	Dansk	Norsk	Svensk

Basics

English	Danish	Norwegian	Swedish
Do you speak	taler De	snakker De	taler ni
Yes/No	ja/nej	ja/nej	ja/nej
Thank you	tak	takk	tack
You're welcome	vaersagod	vaersagod	vaersagod
Excuse me	undskyld	unnskyld	forlat
Hello	dav	hi	hej
Good day	goddag	god dag	god dag
Good morning	godmorgen	god morgen	god morgen
Good night	godnat	god natt	god natt
Good-bye	farvel	farvel	adjo
Man	mand	man	herre
Woman	kvinde	kvinde	dame
Where is	hvor er	hvor er	var ar
The road to	vejen til	veien til	vagen til
When	hvornar	nar	nar
Open	aaben	apent	oppet
Town hall	radhuset	radhuset	radhuset
Post office	posthuset	postkontoret	postkontoret
Station	banegarden	jernbane	station
Hotel	hotel	hotell	hotell
I'd like	jeg oensker	jeg vil	jag skulle
A room	et vaerelse	et vaerelse	ett rum
Single	enkelt	enkel	enkel
Double	dobbelt	dubbel	dubbel
With bath	med bad	med bad	med bad
Key	noglen	nokkelen	nyckeln
Toilet	toilettet	toalettet	toaletten
Old/new	gammel/ny	gammel/ny	gammal/ny
Tourist office	Turistbureau	Turist Informasjon	Turistbyra

On the Road

English	Danish	Norwegian	Swedish
To the right	til hojre	til hoyre	til hoger
To the left	til venstre	til venstre	til vanster
Straight ahead	lige ud	rett fram	rakt fram
Stop	stop	stopp	stopp
Caution	pas paa	se opp	se upp
Slow	langsom	sakte	sakta
One-way street	ensrettet	envegs-kjoring	enkelriktad
No entry	ingen indkorsel	gjennom-kjoring forbudt	infart forbjuden
Brake	bremse	bremse	broms
Breakdown	motorskade	motorstopp	motorstopp

Car	bil	bil	bil
Fuse	sikring	sikring	sakring
Garage	autovaerksted	bilverksted	bilverkstad
Oil change	skifte olie	skifte olie	byt olja
Parking place	parkerings-plads	parkerings-plass	parkerings-plats
Gas station	benzintank	bensinstasjon	bensinstation
Tire	daek	ring	tack

Geography

Mountain	bjerg	berg	berg
Valley	dal	dal	dal
Lake	so	vann	sjo
Beach	strand	strand	strand
Town	by	by	stad
Church	kirke	kirke	kyrka
Castle	slot, borg	slott	slott
Street	gade	gate	gata
Road	vej	vei	vag
Square	torv, plads	torg, plass	torg, plats
Bridge	bro	bru	bro
Railway	jernbane	jembane	jarnvag
Ferry	faerge	ferje	farja

Numbers	Danish	Norwegian	Swedish
1	en	en	en
2	to	to	tva
3	tre	tre	tre
4	fire	fire	fyra
5	fem	fem	fem
6	seks	seks	sex
7	syv	syv	sju
8	otte	atte	atta
9	ni	ni	nio
10	ti	ti	tio
11	elleve	eleeve	elva
12	tolv	tolv	tolv
13	tretten	tretten	tretton
14	fjorten	fjorten	fjorton
15	femten	femten	femton
16	seksten	seksten	sexton
17	sytten	sytten	sjutton
18	atten	atten	arton
19	nitten	nitten	nitton
20	tyve	tjue	tjugo
21	enogtyve	tjue en	tjugo en
22	toogtyve	tjue to	tjugo tva
30	tredive	tretti	trettio
40	fyrre	forti	fyrtio
50	halvtreds	femti	femtio
60	tres	seksti	sextio

70	halvfjerds	sytti	sjuttio
80	firs	atti	attio
90	halvfems	nitti	nittio
100	hundrede	hundre	hundra
200	to hundrede	to hundre	tva hundra
1000	tusind	tusen	tusen

Eating & Drinking

Breakfast	morgenmad	frokost	frukost
Lunch	middagsmad	middagsmat	lunch
Dinner	aftensmad	koeldsmat	middag
Eat	spise	spise	ata
Drink	drikke	frikke	dricka
Many	mange	mye	mycket
A little	lidt	lite	litet
The bill	regning	regning	nota
Pay	betale	betale	betala
Menu	spisekort	spiseseddel	matsedel
Fried	stegt	stekt	stekt
Boiled	kogt	kokt	kokt

Soup	suppe	suppe	soppa
Meat	kod	kjott	kott
Calf	kalv	kalv	kalv
Lamb	lam	lam	lam
Reindeer	ren	rein	ren
Ham	skinke	skinke	skinka
Pig	svin	svin	gris
Sausage	polse	polse	korv
Fish	fisk	fisk	fisk
Cod	torsk	torsk	torsk
Salmon	laks	laks	lax
Shrimp	reje	reke	raka
Trout	orred	orret	forell
Bread	brod	brod	brod
Cake	kage	kake	kaka
Vegetables	gronsager	fronnsaker	gronsaker
Beans	bonne	bonne	bonor
Cauliflower	blomkal	blomkal	blomkal
Green salad	gron salat	hodesalat	gronsallad
Peas	aert	ert	arta
Potatoes	kartoffel	potet	potatis
Fruit	frugt	frukt	frukt
Apple	aeble	eple	apple
Cranberry	tyttebaer	tyttebaer	lingon
Strawberry	jordbaer	jordbaer	jordgubbe
Beer	ol	ol	ol
Coffee	kaffe	kaffe	kaffe
Cream	flode	flote	gradde
Milk	maelk	melk	mjolk
Mineral water	mineralvand	mineralvann	mineralvatten

Tea	te	te	te
Water	vand	vann	vatten
Wine	vin	vin	vin

Dates and Time

The Months: januar, februar, marts, april, maj, juni, juli, august, september, oktober, november, december.
The Days (Sunday-Saturday): sondag, mandag, tirsdag, onsdag, torsdag, fredag, lordag.

Finnish/Suomalainen: Yes—niin; No—en; Thanks—kiitos; Good-bye—nakemiin; Hello—hyvaa paivaa; What does it cost?—Paljonko maksaa?

Scandinavian Climate Chart

1st line, avg. daily low; 2nd line, avg. daily high; 3rd line, days of no rain

	J	F	M	A	M	J	J	A	S	O	N	D
DENMARK Copenhagen												
	29°	28°	31°	37°	44°	51°	55°	54°	49°	42°	35°	32°
	36°	36°	41°	50°	61°	67°	72°	69°	63°	53°	43°	38°
	22	21	23	21	23	22	22	19	22	22	20	20
FINLAND Helsinki												
	17°	15°	22°	31°	41°	49°	58°	55°	46°	37°	30°	22°
	27°	26°	32°	43°	55°	63°	71°	66°	57°	45°	37°	31°
	20	20	23	22	23	21	23	19	19	19	19	20
NORWAY Oslo												
	20°	20°	25°	34°	43°	51°	56°	53°	45°	37°	29°	24°
	30°	32°	40°	50°	62°	69°	73°	69°	60°	49°	37°	31°
	23	21	24	23	24	22	21	20	22	21	21	21
SWEDEN Stockholm												
	23°	22°	26°	32°	41°	49°	55°	53°	46°	39°	31°	26°
	31°	31°	37°	45°	57°	65°	70°	66°	58°	48°	38°	33°
	23	21	24	24	23	23	22	21	22	22	21	22

INDEX

Other Books from John Muir Publications

Adventure Vacations: From Trekking in New Guinea to Swimming in Siberia, Richard Bangs (65-76-9) 256 pp. $17.95

Asia Through the Back Door, 3rd ed., Rick Steves and John Gottberg (65-48-3) 326 pp. $15.95

Being a Father: Family, Work, and Self, *Mothering* Magazine (65-69-6) 176 pp. $12.95

Buddhist America: Centers, Retreats, Practices, Don Morreale (28-94-X) 400 pp. $12.95

Bus Touring: Charter Vacations, U.S.A., Stuart Warren with Douglas Bloch (28-95-8) 168 pp. $9.95

California Public Gardens: A Visitor's Guide, Eric Sigg (65-56-4) 304 pp. $16.95

Catholic America: Self-Renewal Centers and Retreats, Patricia Christian-Meyer (65-20-3) 325 pp. $13.95

Complete Guide to Bed & Breakfasts, Inns & Guesthouses, 1991-92, Pamela Lanier (65-43-2) 520 pp. $16.95

Costa Rica: A Natural Destination, Ree Strange Sheck (65-51-3) 280 pp. $15.95

Elderhostels: The Students' Choice, Mildred Hyman (65-28-9) 224 pp. $12.95 (2nd ed. available 5/91 $15.95)

Environmental Vacations: Volunteer Projects to Save the Planet, Stephanie Ocko (65-78-5) 240 pp. $15.95

Europe 101: History & Art for the Traveler, 4th ed., Rick Steves and Gene Openshaw (65-79-3) 372 pp. $15.95

Europe Through the Back Door, 9th ed., Rick Steves (65-42-4) 432 pp. $16.95

Floating Vacations: River, Lake, and Ocean Adventures, Michael White (65-32-7) 256 pp. $17.95

Gypsying After 40: A Guide to Adventure and Self-Discovery, Bob Harris (28-71-0) 264 pp. $14.95

The Heart of Jerusalem, Arlynn Nellhaus (28-79-6) 336 pp. $12.95

Indian America: A Traveler's Companion, Eagle/Walking Turtle (65-29-7) 424 pp. $16.95 (2nd ed. available 7/91 $16.95)

Mona Winks: Self-Guided Tours of Europe's Top Museums, Rick Steves and Gene Openshaw (28-85-0) 456 pp. $14.95

Opera! The Guide to Western Europe's Great Houses, Karyl Lynn Zietz (65-81-5) 280 pp. $18.95 (Available 4/91)

Paintbrushes and Pistols: How the Taos Artists Sold the West, Sherry C. Taggett and Ted Schwarz (65-65-3) 280 pp. $17.95

The People's Guide to Mexico, 8th ed., Carl Franz (65-60-2) 608 pp. $17.95

The People's Guide to RV Camping in Mexico, Carl Franz with Steve Rogers (2P 91-5) 320 pp. $13.95

Preconception: A Woman's Guide to Preparing for Pregnancy and Parenthood, Brenda E. Aikey-Keller (65-44-0) 232 pp. $14.95

Ranch Vacations: The Complete Guide to Guest and Resort, Fly-Fishing, and Cross-Country Skiing Ranches, Eugene Kilgore (65-30-0) 392 pp. $18.95 (2nd ed. available 5/91 $18.95)

Schooling at Home: Parents, Kids, and Learning, *Mothering* Magazine (65-52-1) 264 pp. $14.95

The Shopper's Guide to Art and Crafts in the Hawaiian Islands, Arnold Schuchter (65-61-0) 272 pp. $13.95

The Shopper's Guide to Mexico, Steve Rogers and Tina Rosa (28-90-7) 224 pp. $9.95

Ski Tech's Guide to Equipment, Skiwear, and Accessories, edited by Bill Tanler (65-45-9) 144 pp. $11.95

Ski Tech's Guide to Maintenance and Repair, edited by Bill Tanler (65-46-7) 160 pp. $11.95

Teens: A Fresh Look, *Mothering* Magazine (65-54-8) 240 pp. $14.95

A Traveler's Guide to Asian Culture, Kevin Chambers (65-14-9) 224 pp. $13.95

Traveler's Guide to Healing Centers and Retreats in North America, Martine Rudee and Jonathan Blease (65-15-7) 240 pp. $11.95

Understanding Europeans, Stuart Miller (65-77-7) 272 pp. $14.95

Undiscovered Islands of the Caribbean, 2nd ed., Burl Willes (65-55-6) 232 pp. $14.95

Undiscovered Islands of the Mediterranean, Linda Lancione Moyer and Burl Willes (65-53-X) 232 pp. $14.95

A Viewer's Guide to Art: A Glossary of Gods, People, and Creatures, Marvin S. Shaw and Richard Warren (65-66-1) 152 pp. $10.95

2 to 22 Days Series

These pocket-size itineraries (4½" × 8") are a refreshing departure from ordinary guidebooks. Each offers 22 flexible daily itineraries that can be used to get the most out of vacations of any length. Included are not only "must see" attractions but also little-known villages and hidden "jewels" as well as valuable general information.

22 Days Around the World, Roger Rapoport and Burl Willes (65-31-9) 200 pp. $9.95 (1992 ed. available 8/91 $11.95)

2 to 22 Days Around the Great Lakes, 1991 ed., Arnold Schuchter (65-62-9) 176 pp. $9.95

22 Days in Alaska, Pamela Lanier (28-68-0) 128 pp. $7.95

22 Days in the American Southwest, 2nd ed., Richard Harris (28-88-5) 176 pp. $9.95

22 Days in Asia, Roger Rapoport and Burl Willes (65-17-3) 136 pp. $7.95 (1992 ed. available 8/91 $9.95)

22 Days in Australia, 3rd ed., John Gottberg (65-40-8) 148 pp. $7.95 (1992 ed. available 8/91 $9.95)

22 Days in California, 2nd ed., Roger Rapoport (65-64-5) 176 pp. $9.95

22 Days in China, Gaylon Duke and Zenia Victor (28-72-9) 144 pp. $7.95

22 Days in Europe, 5th ed., Rick Steves (65-63-7) 192 pp. $9.95

22 Days in Florida, Richard Harris (65-27-0) 136 pp. $7.95 (1992 ed. available 8/91 $9.95)

22 Days in France, Rick Steves (65-07-6) 154 pp. $7.95 (1991 ed. available 4/91 $9.95)

22 Days in Germany, Austria & Switzerland, 3rd ed., Rick Steves (65-39-4) 136 pp. $7.95

22 Days in Great Britain, 3rd ed., Rick Steves (65-38-6) 144 pp. $7.95 (1991 ed. available 4/91 $9.95)

22 Days in Hawaii, 2nd ed., Arnold Schuchter (65-50-5) 144 pp. $7.95 (1992 ed. available 8/91 $9.95)

22 Days in India, Anurag Mathur (28-87-7) 136 pp. $7.95

22 Days in Japan, David Old (28-73-7) 136 pp. $7.95

22 Days in Mexico, 2nd ed., Steve Rogers and Tina Rosa (65-41-6) 128 pp. $7.95

22 Days in New England, Anne Wright (28-96-6) 128 pp. $7.95 (1991 ed. available 4/91 $9.95)

2 to 22 Days in New Zealand, 1991 ed., Arnold Schuchter (65-58-0) 176 pp. $9.95

22 Days in Norway, Sweden, & Denmark, Rick Steves (28-83-4) 136 pp. $7.95 (1991 ed. available 4/91 $9.95)

22 Days in the Pacific Northwest, Richard Harris (28-97-4) 136 pp. $7.95 (1991 ed. available 4/91 $9.95)

22 Days in the Rockies, Roger Rapoport (65-68-8) 176 pp. $9.95

22 Days in Spain & Portugal, 3rd ed., Rick Steves (65-06-8) 136 pp. $7.95

22 Days in Texas, Richard Harris (65-47-5) 176 pp. $9.95

22 Days in Thailand, Derk Richardson (65-57-2) 176 pp. $9.95

22 Days in the West Indies, Cyndy Morreale and Sam Morreale (28-74-5)136 pp. $7.95

"Kidding Around" Travel Guides for Young Readers

Written for kids eight years of age and older. Generously illustrated in two colors with imaginative characters and images. An adventure to read and a treasure to keep.

Kidding Around Atlanta, Anne Pedersen (65-35-1) 64 pp. $9.95

Kidding Around Boston, Helen Byers (65-36-X) 64 pp. $9.95

Kidding Around Chicago, Lauren Davis (65-70-X) 64 pp. $9.95

Kidding Around the Hawaiian Islands, Sarah Lovett (65-37-8) 64 pp. $9.95

Kidding Around London, Sarah Lovett (65-24-6) 64 pp. $9.95

Kidding Around Los Angeles, Judy Cash (65-34-3) 64 pp. $9.95

Kidding Around New York City, Sarah Lovett (65-33-5) 64 pp. $9.95
Kidding Around Paris, Rebecca Clay (65-82-3) 64 pp. $9.95 (Available 4/91)
Kidding Around Philadelphia, Rebecca Clay (65-71-8) 64 pp. $9.95
Kidding Around San Francisco, Rosemary Zibart (65-23-8) 64 pp. $9.95
Kidding Around Santa Fe, Susan York (65-99-8) 64 pp. $9.95 (Available 5/91)
Kidding Around Seattle, Rick Steves (65-84-X) 64 pp. $9.95 (Available 4/91)
Kidding Around Washington, D.C., Anne Pedersen (65-25-4) 64 pp. $9.95

Environmental Books for Young Readers

Written for kids eight years and older. Examines the environmental issues and opportunities that today's kids will face during their lives.

The Indian Way: Learning to Communicate with Mother Earth, Gary McLain (65-73-4) 114 pp. $9.95
The Kids' Environment Book: What's Awry and Why, Anne Pedersen (55-74-2) 192 pp. $13.95
No Vacancy: The Kids' Guide to Population and the Environment, Glenna Boyd (61-000-7) 64 pp. $9.95 (Available 8/91)
Rads, Ergs, and Cheeseburgers: The Kids' Guide to Energy and the Environment, Bill Yanda (65-75-0) 108 pp. $12.95

"Extremely Weird" Series for Young Readers

Written for kids eight years of age and older. Designed to help kids appreciate the world around them. Each book includes full-color photographs with detailed and entertaining descriptions.

Extremely Weird Bats, Sarah Lovett (61-008-2) 48 pp. $9.95 paper (Available 6/91)
Extremely Weird Frogs, Sarah Lovett (61-006-6) 48 pp. $9.95 paper (Available 6/91)
Extremely Weird Spiders, Sarah Lovett (61-007-4) 48 pp. $9.95 paper (Available 6/91)

Automotive Repair Manuals

How to Keep Your VW Alive, 14th ed., (65-80-7) 440 pp. $19.95
How to Keep Your Subaru Alive (65-11-4) 480 pp. $19.95
How to Keep Your Toyota Pickup Alive (28-81-3) 392 pp. $19.95
How to Keep Your Datsun/Nissan Alive (28-65-6) 544 pp. $19.95

Other Automotive Books

The Greaseless Guide to Car Care Confidence: Take the Terror Out of Talking to Your Mechanic, Mary Jackson (65-19-X) 224 pp. $14.95

Off-Road Emergency Repair & Survival, James Ristow (65-26-2) 160 pp. $9.95

Ordering Information

If you cannot find our books in your local bookstore, you can order directly from us. Please check the "Available" date above. If you send us money for a book not yet available, we will hold your money until we can ship you the book. Your books will be sent to you via UPS (for U.S. destinations). UPS will not deliver to a P.O. Box; please give us a street address. Include $2.75 for the first item ordered and $.50 for each additional item to cover shipping and handling costs. For airmail within the U.S., enclose $4.00. All foreign orders will be shipped surface rate; please enclose $3.00 for the first item and $1.00 for each additional item. Please inquire about foreign airmail rates.

Method of Payment

Your order may be paid by check, money order, or credit card. We cannot be responsible for cash sent through the mail. All payments must be made in U.S. dollars drawn on a U.S. bank. Canadian postal money orders in U.S. dollars are acceptable. For VISA, MasterCard, or American Express orders, include your card number, expiration date, and your signature, or call (800) 888-7504. Books ordered on American Express cards can be shipped only to the billing address of the cardholder. Sorry, no C.O.D.'s. Residents of sunny New Mexico, add 5.875% tax to the total.

Address all orders and inquiries to:
John Muir Publications
P.O. Box 613
Santa Fe, NM 87504
(505) 982-4078
(800) 888-7504